WEHRMACHT

The illustrated history of the German Army in WWII

WEHRMACHT

The illustrated history of the German Army in WWII

Dr John Pimlott

AURUM PRESS

First published in Great Britain 1997
by Aurum Press Ltd, 25 Bedford Avenue, London WC1B 3AT
© 1997 Brown Packaging Books Ltd

A catalogue record for this book is available from the British Library.

ISBN 1 85410 465 9

1 2 3 4 5 6 7 8 9 10

1997 1998 1999 2000 2001

Conceived and produced by Brown Packaging Books Ltd
Editor: Peter Darman
Design: wda

Produced in cooperation with Espadon Books Ltd, Warsaw, Poland

Printed and bound in Italy

Page 1: A Wehrmacht cameraman and his comrade, armed with a Steyr-Solothurn S1-100 submachine gun.
Page 2: German infantry attack a Belgian town in May 1940. The machine gun is a schwere Maschinengewehr (MG) 34 mounted on a tripod.

CONTENTS

CHAPTER 1

BIRTH OF THE BLITZKRIEG

Following the humiliation of defeat in World War I, the German Army was seemingly emasculated by the Treaty of Versailles. Yet within 20 years it had been rebuilt, and under the Nazis was ready to fight a new type of war.

Left: Adolf Hitler (1889-1945), Chancellor of Germany from 1933 until his suicide in the ruins of Berlin in April 1945.

Above: Members of the Sturmabteilung (SA) – the Nazi Party's 'private army' – participate in a public rally in the early 1930s.

At 1100 hours on 11 November 1918 the guns fell silent on the Western Front after more than four years of bitter and costly war. Despite claims made later by Adolf Hitler that the Armistice was forced on the Germans by corrupt politicians and that the German Army was undefeated in battle, the reality was far more severe. After the failure of General Erich Ludendorff's Spring 1918 Offensive, the Allied powers had gradually assumed the initiative, forcing the Germans back almost to their own borders. With a catastrophic military defeat staring them in the face and society in Germany on the point of collapse under the twin pressures of food shortages and spreading Bolshevik unrest, there was little choice but to seek an end to the fighting. The German Army may have marched home with flags flying, but it was no longer capable of defending the state against foreign invaders.

Above: German infantry under training in the late 1930s. Lightly equipped and armed with Mauser 98 bolt-action rifles, these are successors to the Stosstruppen (Stormtroopers) of 1918, capable of rapid movement designed to infiltrate enemy positions prior to the main assault.

Nevertheless, the Imperial German Army, with its roots in the Prussian militarism of the late eighteenth century and a proud record of battlefield success since its formation under the Kaiser in 1871, was still potentially a formidable force. More than three million men remained under arms in the west and the army's superbly organised Great General Staff survived. However, the victorious Allies were intent on reducing the army and preventing its resurgence.

On 28 June 1919, when German representatives were given no choice but to sign the Treaty of Versailles, stringent terms were laid down. Germany was held to blame for the 'Great War' and obliged to pay swingeing reparations that were guaranteed to prevent economic revival and the creation of the means to wage war in the future. More significantly, the size of her armed forces was cut to derisory levels. The navy was reduced to the status of a coastal protection force, while the army was restricted to 100,000 men, responsible for home defence only. Moreover, the weapons available were curtailed: the navy was not allowed to build or acquire capital ships, and the army was allowed no tanks, heavy artillery or air support. In addition, the Great General Staff, seen by many Allied leaders as a major source of German militarism before 1914, was disbanded, as were many of the cadet schools

Right: An Oberkanonier (Senior Artillery Soldier), denoted by the woven star on his left sleeve, practises sighting his weapon under gas conditions during an exercise. All German soldiers carried a gas mask in a distinctive metal canister, usually slung over the shoulder on a leather strap.

and military academies. The intention was to emasculate Germany and leave it vulnerable to pressure from surrounding powers, so ensuring its continued weakness.

To an extent, this was unnecessary, as the army had effectively disbanded itself in early 1919. When the soldiers returned to Germany, many were stunned by the social and political upheavals in the state and wanted nothing more than to return home. Others, kept on by authorities wary of the spread of Bolshevism, openly discussed mutiny, organising Soldiers' Councils which insisted on control over demobilization and an end to all privileges of officer rank. The abdication of the Kaiser in November 1918, just prior to the Armistice, left many officers unsure of their loyalties, and for a time it looked as if Germany would degenerate into revolution, following the pattern established in Russia in 1917.

The Freikorps

The new German republic was desperate for some sort of internal protection, so it turned to right-wing volunteer units known as the Freikorps, established by army officers and soldiers who were intent on preventing the spread of revolution. To begin with, these units emerged spontaneously, lacking both central direction and, in many cases, proper discipline, but they were the only

Below: German anti-tank gunners manoeuvre a 37mm Panzerabwehrkanone 37(t) into position. The Pak 37(t), shown here with its early wooden spoked wheels, was originally of Czech manufacture. Stocks of such weapons were captured in 1939 and became standard issue for German units.

coherent force available. Trusted officers were sent to try to control the Freikorps, to the extent that, by 1921, when the new Reichswehr (armed force) was set up, the Freikorps units made up the bulk of the 100,000-man Reichsheer (army). Links with the old Imperial Army were therefore tenuous; the Weimar Republic was effectively starting from scratch, creating a home defence force in line with the Versailles Treaty.

The shaping of the Reichsheer

But some traditions remained. General Hans von Seeckt, appointed by the Weimar authorities to head the Reichsheer, used his position to create an effective force within the parameters laid down. Thus, although the Allies had insisted on the disbandment of the Great General Staff, von Seeckt set up an organization with virtually similar duties under the title of Truppenamt, and did so in ways that actually made it much more centralized and potentially very strong.

At the same time, the 4000 officers permitted under Versailles were carefully chosen, often on their war records, so that dead wood was cut out and the officer corps became much more effectively professional. In the same way, soldiers to man the two army corps that were allowed – one in Berlin and the other in Kassel – were taken from a pool of experienced and willing volunteers, the

Below: Infantry on exercise, mid-1930s. Armed with stick-grenades and 7.92mm Mauser Gewehr 98 rifles – the standard service rifle of World War I. Some of the soldiers are still wearing old-style helmets and footwear. This suggests a photograph taken in about 1935, as the new conscripts are being trained.

Above: A soldier negotiates a barbed-wire obstacle, using methods reminiscent of World War I; indeed, the wirecutters he is using are probably a relic from that conflict. Although barbed-wire would never be as important once mechanization took hold, it was still a simple and effective barrier to infantry.

majority of whom would, in previous generations, have made ideal non-commissioned officers. Von Seeckt even insisted on transferring traditions and identities from the Imperial Army to the new force in an effort to instil pride. Without the Allies noticing, the Reichsheer emerged as a tight, efficient nucleus, capable of future expansion.

In order to satisfy the Allies, von Seeckt made every effort to ensure that the new Reichsheer remained aloof from the politics of the state, but this did not prevent him from allowing his more dynamic officers to conduct experiments designed to improve the military skills of the force. In 1922, as the Weimar authorities began to search for potential allies in a hostile world, the Treaty of Rapallo was signed with the Soviet Union, ostensibly to contain any threat from Poland. As part of the agreement, the Reichsheer

Above: The Wehrmacht was not the only military organization in Germany in the 1930s training for war. This mortar crew consists of members of the armed SS, the Waffen-SS (shown by the arm-eagle). The man in the foreground is wearing police insignia on his helmet.

gained the right, hidden from the Versailles powers, to train selected officers and soldiers in the use of tanks and aircraft, provided by the Russians at secret locations at Kazan and Lipetsk. In return, the Germans passed on technical and tactical expertise.

Also in this period, von Seeckt recognized the potential of mechanization, and although this was never to affect the army as a whole – as late as 1945, the Wehrmacht was still essentially horse-drawn – it did allow officers such as Heinz Guderian, a signals

Above: The crew of a schwerer Panzerspahwagen (Sd Kfz) 231 armoured car prepare to mount, prior to carrying out a reconnaissance mission in wooded terrain. Armed with a 20mm gun and a machine gun, the Sd Kfz 231 was introduced in 1938, principally to act as the 'eyes' of a panzer division.

specialist who transferred to the Inspectorate of Mechanized Troops in the 1920s, to conduct experiments that would eventually lead to the creation of the all-arm panzer divisions. During the 1920s and early 1930s, experience with tanks could be gained at Kazan, although in Germany the experiments had to be conducted with agricultural tractors or automobiles disguised to look like tanks. This may have seemed ridiculous to onlookers, but it succeeded in familiarizing soldiers with the intricacies of armoured warfare, which proved invaluable.

Thus, when Hitler came to power in Germany in 1933, he inherited an army that, despite its size, was dynamic and aware of the latest ideas (many of them culled from the writings of British, French and Russian officers who had taken time to analyze the lessons of the recent war, not least in terms of the tank). Hitler had

been a front-line soldier during the Great War – his Iron Cross First Class was won for bravery in the field and was not a common award to an ordinary soldier – and soon displayed his intention to expand the size of the army in direct contravention of the Versailles Treaty. In December 1933, for example, he ordered a threefold increase to the force, aiming to field 21 divisions by 1938, and in March 1935 he went further, reintroducing conscription and calling for an army of no less than 36 divisions. By then,

Left: A Panzerkampfwagen (Pz Kpfw) III, photographed in combat conditions. Armed with a 37mm or (as shown) a 50mm main gun and two 7.92mm machine guns, the Pz Kpfw III was the first German tank to go into mass production, entering service just prior to the invasion of Poland in September 1939.

sion that Germany's defence minister should never be a serving officer, von Blomberg remained in post from 1932 until his dismissal in 1938. It was he who began the process of politicizing the Wehrmacht (as the Reichswehr was renamed in 1935), chiefly in response to the existence of the Nazis' own 'private army', the Sturmabteilung (SA), under the leadership of Ernst Röhm, and to growing demands from Hermann Göring, as head of the Luftwaffe, for independence of command.

The Führer's Wehrmacht

Von Blomberg ordered that Nazi Party insignia be worn on all uniforms, and the process culminated in August 1934 with the introduction of a new oath of allegiance, sworn by every serving soldier and future recruit, which radically altered the place of the armed forces in the German state. Instead of swearing allegiance to the constitution, officers and men were ordered to swear unconditional obedience to Adolf Hitler as 'the Führer of the German Reich'. As events in July 1944 were to show, when an attempt was made to assassinate Hitler, many officers regarded this oath as sacrosanct and refused, despite their misgivings, to openly oppose their chosen Führer. It gave Hitler unprecedented influence over the Wehrmacht, reinforced in 1938 when von Blomberg was sacked and Hitler made himself War Minister.

an announcement had also been made that Germany would recreate the Luftwaffe (air force), with no restrictions on the types of aircraft available. Britain and France, weakened by economic and political crises, did nothing to prevent such a resurgence of German military power.

Conscription gave the German Army its recruits, but it was still theoretically an apolitical force, removed from the machinations of politics. Hitler, aware that his policies would involve him in territorial expansion, needed to ensure that the armed forces as a whole would be available to carry out such policies unquestioningly. In this, he was aided by his Minister of Defence, General of Infantry Werner von Blomberg. Despite a Versailles Treaty provi-

Also in 1938, the former Truppenamt was transformed into the Oberkommando der Wehrmacht (OKW) under General of Artillery Wilhelm Keitel, a notoriously pro-Nazi officer, and the Army General Staff was effectively reformed as the

Right: German gunners fire a schwere Kanone 18 in action, 1939. Developed between 1926 and 1929 by Krupp and Rheinmetall, the 100mm K 18 was accepted for issue to artillery units in 1933-34. It remained in production until 1943, having seen widespread active duty throughout the early blitzkrieg campaigns. It was a powerful weapon.

Left: Anti-tank gunners man-handle a 37mm Pak 37(t) into position. The provision of anti-tank weapons to infantry units was essential for mechanized warfare, although as tank design improved, guns of greater hitting power had to be evolved. By the standards of 1942, for example, the Pak 37(t) was a peashooter.

Below: Infantry fire a 7.92mm Maschinengewehr 34 machine gun. Designed in the early 1930s and accepted for production in 1934, the MG 34 was the standard German machine gun of the early years of World War II. With a cyclic rate of fire of 900 rounds per minute, it was an extremely effective weapon.

Oberkommando des Heeres (OKH) under a new Commander-in-Chief, General of Artillery Walter von Brauchitsch. Relations between OKW and OKH were never good, and Hitler was able to exploit their differences to ensure his personal control.

By then, the Wehrmacht had expanded in size considerably. Most of the new conscripts found themselves in the infantry, the basic organization of which had not changed dramatically since the Great War. Infantry divisions remained at three regiments each, with integral artillery and engineer support, and although some motor transport was provided, the soldiers were expected to march into battle in their jackboots. Much of the artillery was still horse-drawn, as were the bulk of the supply columns. However, mechanization was pursued in the newly formed panzer (armoured) divisions, developed principally by Guderian. He had read many of the papers and books produced by theorists such as Basil Liddell Hart and J.F.C. Fuller in Britain, and although their influence has been substantially over-emphasized – Guderian proved quite capable of working out ideas for himself – the common denominator of the impact of the tank and its supporting arms was apparent.

The theory of the blitzkrieg

Officers such as Guderian quickly realized that the tank offered great potential in terms of restoring mobility to the battlefield, although not on its own. It needed to be part of an all-arms formation, comprising mechanized infantry, mobile artillery and engineers, and required close support from the air, if it was to act as a spearhead capable of finding and exploiting lines of least resis-

tance in enemy defences, prior to deep penetrations which would destroy the enemy's cohesion as a fighting force. If, for example, the panzers, deliberately avoiding enemy strongpoints and concentrations, could lance through the frontline to hit enemy command and control functions, severing the links between the enemy army's 'brain' and its front-line 'muscle', that 'muscle' would wither and die, precluding the need for the sort of attri-

Above: An infantry section, armed with 7.92mm Mauser 98 rifles and an MG 34 machinegun, negotiate a small stream; the section leader on the right is carrying a Stielhandgranate 39 grenade. The obvious lack of concern about possible enemy positions on the far bank suggests an exercise.

tional battles that had produced such heavy casualties in the Great War. It was a visionary scheme, and one that caught Hitler's imagination. It was later to gain notoriety under the journalistic title of blitzkrieg (lightning war).

Hitler's enthusiasm ensured a release of funds to allow experiments to continue, culminating in 1935 with the creation of the first three panzer divisions. These were potentially effective formations, containing regiments of tanks for punch and speed, motorized infantry for protection, towed artillery for concentrated firepower and combat engineers for obstacle clearance. In addition, Göring was persuaded to devote the bulk of the Luftwaffe to ground support, including the Junkers Ju-87 Stuka dive-bomber, deliberately used as a weapon that would demoralize enemy troops prior to a panzer attack. It was a formidable combination,

Above: German troops in Spain, supporting Franco's Nationalists in the civil war, advance through a village in Catalonia, 1938. The motorcyclists are riding on BMW R11 combinations, designed for reconnaissance; in the background are Pz Kpfw I tanks – better than anything in Republican hands.

although even at this early stage it contained two flaws that were later to prove fatal.

First, despite Hitler's approval, the panzer divisions were only a very small part of the Wehrmacht – the original three divisions had only been increased to seven by 1939 – leaving the bulk of the army still dependent on the foot-borne infantryman who, by definition, would soon lag far behind the mobile spearheads. Secondly, the equipment with which the panzers were issued in the late 1930s took time to develop, with the result that early panzers such as the Mark I and Mark II were too small and lightly armed to be effective. They might have been capable of a decent turn of speed, but the Mark I was armed with machine guns only and the Mark II with no more than a very light cannon, incapable of penetrating armour plate. Equipment would improve as Hitler prepared for, then initiated, the next major war, but the gap between the capabilities of infantry and panzers would bedevil the Wehrmacht until its eventual defeat in 1945.

Putting theory into practice

None of this was apparent in the late 1930s, as Hitler flexed his military muscles to overturn the Versailles conditions and expand the territory of the Third Reich. As early as 1936 he sent forces into the 'demilitarized' Rhineland, eliciting no response from the British or French; two years later he engineered an Anschluss (union) with Austria and regained the Sudetenland from Czechoslovakia, with Anglo-French approval at the Munich conference; in March 1939 he openly invaded the remaining part of Czechoslovakia. In all cases, his forces were spearheaded by the panzer divisions and covered by the Luftwaffe, helping to create an image of modern, terrifyingly capable armed might.

This image was enhanced by German involvement in the Spanish Civil War (1936–39), where panzers and Luftwaffe aircraft practised their art – the latter notoriously by bombing Guernica in 1937, heightening fears of German civilian bombing in the event of a major war with Britain and France – while the blatant use of the Wehrmacht to support the Nazi cause at Party rallies, deliberately orchestrated to project both power and prestige, did nothing to persuade observers that Germany was anything other than immensely strong. In retrospect, this may be seen to have been something of a façade, but by the late summer of 1939, as European relations deteriorated to the point of war over German demands on Poland, few would have doubted that the Wehrmacht was a frightening instrument of power. As events unfolded in Europe during the next two years, this impression was not to be undermined.

Right: Hitler, riding in a Mercedes staff car, shows himself to enthusiastic crowds in Vienna after the Anschluss of 1938. His politically engineered union between Austria (the country of his birth) and Germany created a bloc of territory in central Europe that set alarm bells ringing in neighbouring countries.

Below: A German artillery ammunition column (note the absence of guns) moves into the Austrian frontier town of Kufstein in March 1938, immediately after the announcement of the Anschluss. The crowds are welcoming, many of them waving Nazi flags. Horse-drawn columns were to remain an anachronistic feature of the Wehrmacht until 1945.

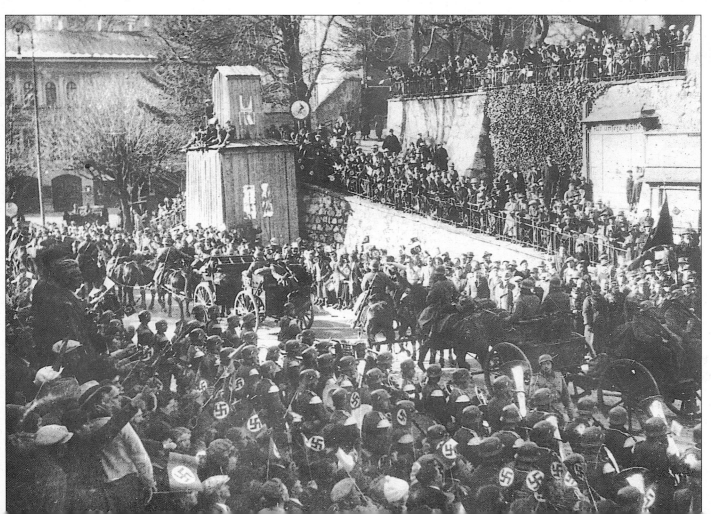

CHAPTER 2

LIGHTNING STRIKES

It took less than a month for the German Army to destroy its Polish counterpart in September 1939, and by June 1940 it had conquered Norway, the Low Countries and France in a series of stunning campaigns.

Left: An infantry lieutenant orders his men to halt as they enter a small town in Poland, September 1939.

Above: 1 September 1939: German units pour into western Poland, their supply vehicles stretching as far as the eye can see.

Hitler's invasion of Poland began at dawn on 1 September 1939, when German aircraft carried out a series of pre-emptive strikes against Polish airfields in an attempt to gain air superiority. As the bombers and fighter-bombers returned to their bases, ground forces totalling over 1.5 million men, 2500 tanks and nearly 10,000 artillery pieces crossed the border. They were divided into two separate formations: Army Group North (General

Fedor von Bock) in Pomerania and East Prussia, tasked with squeezing out the 'Polish Corridor' to Danzig and threatening Warsaw from the north, and Army Group South (General Gerd von Rundstedt) in Silesia and Slovakia, tasked with destroying Polish units protecting Warsaw from the west and south. Their opponents in the Polish Army – one million men, equipped with 475 tanks and 2800 artillery pieces – were badly deployed close to

Above: German troops, helped by border guards, break down a frontier post between Germany and Poland on 1 September 1939. Images such as these brought it home to Poland's allies in the west that Germany meant business. Britain and France declared war on Germany two days later, widening the war.

Right: A lieutenant prepares to brief his men just prior to an assault on the defences around Warsaw in September 1939. The strain of campaigning is beginning to tell, not just on the facial expressions of the soldiers but also on their uniforms, which are starting to lose their peacetime gloss.

Above: *A formation of Pz Kpfw I Ausf B light tanks of the 1st Panzer Division move forward through the dust of western Poland, early September 1939. The white crosses on the tanks are recognition symbols used just for the Polish campaign; they would soon be replaced by the more familiar black crosses lined with white (they made good aiming marks for anti-tank gunners!).*

Below: *As Polish units withdraw in the face of the German blitzkrieg, they try desperately to block the roads. Here an Sd Kfz 231 armoured car, with motorcycle escort, is waiting for the road to be cleared by what appear to be civilians. Such obstacles did little to prevent the German advance, though, as their armour swept all before them.*

the border areas and lacked inherent mobility. They had little choice but to stand and fight where they were, while remaining constantly aware that the Soviets, now in alliance with Hitler, posed a potential threat from the east.

The Polish campaign

The ensuing campaign was short and decisive. In the north, the Polish Corridor was breached by 5 September, linking Pomerania and East Prussia for the first time since 1920, and Roznan was taken on the same day, opening the way towards Brest-Litovsk. Further south, von Rundstedt encountered some Polish resistance on the River Bzura, but by mid-September had managed to encircle the main enemy formations both there and close to Krakow. What remained of Polish forces collapsed once the Soviets opened their attack from the east. On 27 September Warsaw was taken, having been subjected to deliberate 'terror-bombing' by the Luftwaffe, and Poland was split between Germany and the Soviet Union along the line of the River Bug. In just four weeks of fighting, Poland had been crushed and her allies, Britain and France (both of whom had declared war on Germany on 3 September), left stunned by an awesome display of Wehrmacht power.

Such a victory suited Hitler's war-fighting preferences. The cost may have been quite high – about 15,000 German troops were

Above: Engineers were vital to maintain the momentum of blitzkrieg formations, not least when it came to river-crossings. This bridge, thrown across the River Vistula near Bydgoszcz in September 1939, shows what needed to be achieved, preferably at great speed. Note the original bridge in the background.

killed in Poland and the Luftwaffe lost nearly 500 aircraft destroyed or badly damaged – but they were sustainable as long as the fighting was decisive and of short duration. In addition, the campaign reinforced the view that panzer divisions, supported by aircraft, could open up enemy defences, leading to collapse. Although the Wehrmacht did not practise pure blitzkrieg in Poland – the panzers, for example, were not concentrated but divided out to support essentially infantry advances – the speed and mobility of some of the attacks clearly shocked the Poles, catching them 'wrong-footed' and leaving them incapable of mounting a coherent defence. Small wonder, therefore, that Hitler ordered the creation of additional panzer divisions in late 1939, prior to his next strategic move – attacks in the west.

Ironically, the panzers had little part to play in the first of these attacks – the invasions of Denmark and Norway, triggered on 9 April 1940 under the codename Operation Weserubung. This was a true Wehrmacht campaign, involving elements of all three ser-

Above: German troops snatch a hot meal from a field kitchen, colloquially known as a Gullaschkanone, or 'Goulash Gun'. The photograph was probably taken in Poland in late September 1939, when deteriorating weather necessitated the wearing of greatcoats and ponchos.

Left: Infantry, under the command of the Unteroffizier (non-commissioned officer) on the left, pause for a cigarette break during the early days of the Polish campaign in September 1939. The soldiers all have Stielhandgranate 39 stick grenades in their belts, ready for instant action.

Left: A Polish staff officer (left) discusses terms for the surrender of Warsaw with his German counterpart, 26 September 1939. A civilian representative is also present, indicating that the surrender marks the end of the fighting in Poland. The first of the blitzkrieg campaigns is about to end after less than a month.

Above: Hitler enters Warsaw in triumph on 5 October 1939. Closely guarded by an Sd Kfz 222 reconnaissance car, freshly painted for the occasion, the Führer is being fêted by his own troops, not by the local population. The commander of the escort is wearing the distinctive black Schutzmutze beret, discontinued in early 1940.

Left: An Unteroffizier (right) waits to order his men forward on the outskirts of Warsaw, September 1939. The masts of the Raszyn radio transmitting station can be seen in the background. Shown to advantage is the bayonet for the standard 7.92mm 98K rifle.

vices (navy, air force and army) in an ambitious attempt to seize ports with more direct access to the North Atlantic, where U-Boats and surface warships were already attacking vital Allied trade routes. Substantial forces were deployed – the bulk of the Kriegsmarine (navy) surface fleet, 28 U-Boats, over 500 aircraft and 8 divisions of the army – and new techniques were deployed, including for the first time the use of airlanding and parachute units to seize airfields and other key locations in an effort to disrupt enemy defences.

Initially, all went smoothly. Denmark surrendered on 9 April, principally to avoid threatened bombing raids on Copenhagen, and German troops secured a number of Norwegian objectives, including Narvik, Trondheim, Bergen, Stavanger and Kristiansand, without encountering stiff resistance. But the German enclaves were isolated and, as Britain and France committed forces to aid the Norwegians, the prospect of a stiffer fight emerged. German naval losses quickly mounted, and if it had not been for the seizure of airfields by the airborne troops, enabling transport aircraft to land direct from northern Germany, resupply would have been a major problem.

German gains in Norway

As it was, the Germans were able to consolidate their positions in southern Norway, linking their enclaves at Bergen and Trondheim and seizing Oslo. British units were landed at Namsos on 14 April and Andalsnes four days later in an effort to protect the central part of the country, but they were soon outfought and forced to withdraw. By early May, the Germans were in firm possession of all but the far north, around Narvik. Although the Allies mounted a belated attack on that port on 13 May, pushing the occupiers

Left: A Gebirgsjager (member of the mountain troops) advances along a stream in the difficult terrain of northern Norway, 1940. The issue of bicycles was intended to impart mobility, although in this particular case the need to carry the machine was counter-productive. Note the distinctive high-cut mountain boots.

Left: General Eduard Dietl (1890-1944), commander of German mountain troops involved in the invasion of northern Norway, points accusingly at the camera while on an inspection tour around Narvik in June 1940. His mode of transport is unusual – a horse-drawn railway truck – but practical.

Above: Mountain troops in Norway fire their 80mm Granatwerfer 34 mortar towards enemy positions. The terrain is rugged and the weather cold; one of the results is that the mortar has been positioned with its base-plate on the roadway – not the ideal way to absorb the shock of firing.

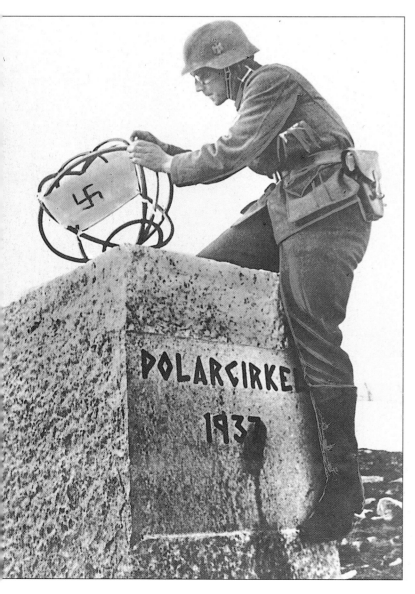

Above: British soldiers, captured during the fighting around Trondheim in April 1940, are escorted to ships that will take them to prisoner of war camps in Germany. They face more than five years in captivity, the unwilling victims of the disastrous Allied strategy in Norway.

Left: A German soldier attaches a Nazi flag to an obelisk denoting the edge of the Arctic Circle in northern Norway, May 1940. The pistol he is wearing appears to be a Polish ViS (or 'Radom') 9mm P35(p), presumably captured in September 1939. The Germans rarely wasted captured weapon stocks.

Right: Narvik after the Allied withdrawal in early June 1940. Important as a port for the movement of Swedish iron ore, the loss of Narvik was a blow to the Allied war effort, but more pressing events were occurring in France and the Low Countries.

out, they proved incapable of holding on to their gains. Narvik was abandoned on 9 June, leaving the Germans in full possession of the country.

As with Poland, the cost to the Wehrmacht had not been small – 5700 dead, plus the loss of 13 warships and 6 U-Boats – but the strategic gains had been substantial and the campaign had lasted only a matter of weeks. A pattern of short, sharp and decisive offensives was beginning to emerge, enhancing the reputation and morale of the Wehrmacht.

This pattern was considerably reinforced by concurrent events in France and the Low Countries, for if Poland and Scandinavia had been impressive campaigns, the German defeat of the main western Allies in May-June 1940 was stunning in its speed and impact. No one in September 1939 would have guessed that the British and French were so vulnerable to German attack. France itself appeared secure behind the formidable defences of the Maginot Line, stretching all along the border with Germany, and had substantial forces available for operations elsewhere, while the British Expeditionary Force (BEF), deployed to France as soon

as the war began, partly made up for its relatively small size (nine divisions) by the fact that it was, unlike the Wehrmacht, fully mechanized.

In all, the Allies were fielding over 100 divisions, more than 2000 tanks and 4000 combat aircraft by the spring of 1940, and seemed secure in their assessment that any German attack would have to come through the Low Countries to avoid both the Maginot Line and the difficult terrain of the Ardennes region. Their plan was to wait until the Germans moved into the Low Countries, upon which they would commit mobile formations north to meet the invaders, blunting their assault.

Allied tactical deficiencies

In itself, this was logical, but the Allied armies were not as strong as they seemed. Coordination between air and ground forces was weak, tanks were 'penny-packeted' in direct support of infantry formations, command arrangements between the Allies were poor and, as the winter of 1939-40 dragged on without any action, troop morale declined. The only boost came in January 1940,

Above: Demoralized Belgian troops surrender to a German unit, May 1940. The Belgian Army, ill-prepared for war, could do little to prevent the advance of Army Group B, despite the support received from elements of the French Army and the British Expeditionary Force. Belgium surrendered on 28 May.

Right: German troops, having left their own transport vehicles under the trees, view the shattered remains of a Belgian artillery column, caught by air attack in the opening stages of the 1940 campaign. The ability of German ground commanders to call down air attacks did much to demoralize their enemies.

Left: Parachute engineers, belonging to the Luftwaffe but with an army colleague on the left, celebrate their seizure of the Belgian fortress at Eben Emael, May 1940. The engineers arrived at the fortress in gliders, landing on the roof to achieve maximum effect. They then used explosives to blast their way in.

when a Luftwaffe aircraft crashed in neutral Belgium and was found to contain a full set of operational plans for Fall Gelb (Plan Yellow), the projected German invasion of the Low Countries. The plans were returned, apparently unopened by the officially neutral Belgians, but their contents had been disseminated to Allied governments. They reinforced existing Allied preconceptions.

This incident was a turning point for the Wehrmacht, for once it was suspected that Fall Gelb had been compromised, Hitler's support for the plan began to wane. He quickly accepted a revised version, known as Sichelschnitt or 'cut of the scythe', put forward by General Erich von Manstein, chief of staff to Army Group A facing Belgium in the east. He suggested an attack by Army Group B in the north to trigger the expected Allied move into Belgium, upon which seven panzer divisions, concentrated for the purpose in Army Group A, would infiltrate the Ardennes and push through

to the Channel coast, cutting the Allied forces now in Belgium off from their support in France and causing their collapse as they faced attacks from two directions simultaneously. Despite severe misgivings expressed by the more traditional generals of OKH, who doubted the ability of the panzers to pass through the Ardennes and cross the barrier of the River Meuse to the west, Hitler saw the opportunity that could arise. The result was a classic blitzkrieg campaign.

As in Poland, the German attack began with pre-emptive air strikes. Early on 10 May 1940, Luftwaffe bombers and fighter-bombers sought out Allied airstrips to destroy as many aircraft as possible on the ground, so securing a measure of air superiority. Simultaneously, ground units of Army Group B (von Bock) crossed the border into the Netherlands and northern Belgium, along what appeared to be the expected avenue of attack, using

airborne troops to seize vital locations (including the key Belgian border fortress of Eben Emael, assaulted by gliderborne engineers) and fielding spearheads comprising three panzer divisions. To the Allies, secure in their knowledge of Fall Gelb, this fitted the expected pattern of events; they triggered their Plan 'D' and moved the bulk of their mobile formations, including the BEF, forward into Belgium, ready for a major meeting engagement along the River Dyle. Reports from the Ardennes that German forces were active in that region were dismissed as a feint.

This gave the concentrated panzers of Army Group A (von Rundstedt) the opportunity they needed. As the Allies looked north, three panzer corps, containing a total of seven panzer divisions, wound their way slowly along narrow roads to approach

the Meuse. Local defenders were pushed aside, aircraft were deployed for forward reconnaissance in the knowledge that Allied air capability had been curtailed by the pre-emptive strikes, and momentum began to build. By late on 12 May, lead units of General Hermann Hoth's XV Panzer Corps reached the Meuse to the north of Dinant without encountering strong opposition and, 24 hours later, General Rommel's 7th Panzer Division was across. To Rommel's south, General Georg-Hans Reinhardt's XLI Panzer Corps and Guderian's XIX Panzer Corps crossed at Monthermé and Sedan respectively on 14/15 May, opening gaps in the French defences that would take them to the Channel in less than six days. The main Allied formations, fixed in Belgium by Army Group B, suddenly found themselves in danger of encirclement.

Left: A Pz Kpfw II of the 5th Panzer Division enters the ruins of Rouen, June 1940, during the final stages of the French defeat. The Dunkirk evacuation has been successfully completed, remaining Allied troops are totally confused and demoralized, French cities have been bombed. Blitzkrieg is working and the French are about to capitulate.

Right: German Sanitätssoldaten (medical personnel) carry a casualty away from the sand dunes at Dunkirk, early June 1940. The man on the stretcher is German rather than Allied, making the point that, regardless of the stunning nature of German victory, it still cost casualties – 137,000 German killed and wounded in just six weeks.

Below: An infantry squad shelters in the walled garden of a house in Tournai in Belgium during the German advance towards the coast in May 1940. Allied artillery, deployed along the Escaut river, is bombarding the area, although none of the soldiers appear to be particularly concerned. The rest is probably welcome.

The Meuse crossings were the key to German success. They were achieved not just because French defences were weak, but because the Wehrmacht was by this stage perfecting many of its techniques. Guderian's crossing at Sedan illustrated the advantages of blitzkrieg. As his lead tanks approached what should have been a major river obstacle, Guderian was able to call on the Luftwaffe to give him reports about enemy defences – something that would have been impossible without air superiority – and when his initial attempts to seize a crossing using just engineers supported by infantry were repulsed, he was able to concentrate all his resources quickly to ensure success.

Tanks were lined up along the east bank of the river to give fire support, Stuka dive-bombers were called in to soften up the enemy positions and, under cover of these attacks, forces were pushed rapidly across to seize a bridgehead. Pontoon bridges were constructed by the engineers so that tanks could cross, and once they appeared among the already battered defenders, the French units broke and ran. Initial surprise among the defenders had been exploited by the momentum of the German assault, itself dependent on a mixture of air superiority and all-arms co-operation, plus of course the dynamic leadership of Guderian himself. Indeed, the main problem he experienced was not the

Below: German troops seek shelter close to the Maginot Line fortifications, June 1940. Their schwere Maschinengewehr 34 heavy machine gun is on a special mounting designed for long-range firing from a solid platform. Also shown by the soldier in the foreground is the gasmask canister.

Right: A German infantryman carries his MG 34 machine gun through barbed-wire entanglements close to a rather crude bunker. The photograph was clearly taken during a pre-war exercise in Germany, although the sort of preparation involved proved useful against the Maginot Line in June 1940.

enemy but congestion along the narrow roads of the Ardennes. This was why his assault did not include artillery, much of which was stuck in traffic jams to the rear.

Once the panzer divisions were across, there was little to prevent their advance through the rear of Allied formations. The distance to the Channel was manageable (about 300km/190 miles) and the Allied response was poor, reflecting their weaknesses of command and coordination. Guderian reached the coast by 20 May, leaving the main Allied armies caught between Army Group B and the panzer spearheads. They had little choice but to pull back towards Dunkirk, where plans were already in train for a naval evacuation. The Netherlands and Luxembourg had both surrendered by this stage; Belgium was to follow suit on 28 May, along with its monarch, King Leopold III.

The fall of France

In the event, over 330,000 Allied troops were rescued from Dunkirk by 4 June, but they left behind all their heavy weapons and any hope of redeploying them to the south of the panzer thrust quickly proved impracticable. In total, the Allies had lost 61 divisions, which was over half their order of battle and the best they possessed. Those remaining divisions which faced the Germans numbered only 49, and were for the most part poorly trained and equipped and totally demoralized. Army Groups A and B joined forces in early June, shifting south to hit the demoralized remnants of the French Army. Paris fell on 14 June; eight days later, the French Government surrendered. For losses of 137,000 men killed and wounded, the Germans had achieved the seemingly impossible – the defeat of all the western Allies in a campaign lasting a mere six weeks.

Below: A 150mm schwere Feldhaubitze 18 at the point of firing, probably during a pre-war exercise. A well trained crew, as shown here, could fire four 150mm shells a minute to a maximum range of 8.28 miles (13,325m), providing sustained and heavy fire support to infantry or armoured units. The impact could be dramatic.

Left: Infantry soldiers, lightly equipped in the best traditions of stormtroopers, rush forward to seize a railway station in rural France, early 1940. The railway system was vital for the movement of supplies and reinforcements; the fact that it was virtually undefended indicates the extent of the Allied collapse.

But problems had occurred. The panzer spearheads achieved a great deal, but they had raced ahead of their follow-up infantry formations, whose foot-slogging progress was slowed even more by the need to consolidate ground and take prisoners. Indeed, Hitler had been aware of this and twice in late May had ordered the panzers to halt while the infantry caught up, decisions which, it could be argued, gave the Allies the breathing space they needed to organize the crucial Dunkirk evacuation. Similarly, logistic difficulties had been experienced by the panzers, as supply columns became ensnarled in the rear-area traffic jams or simply lacked the mobility to keep up. In the event, neither problem proved crucial in this campaign, but when Adolf Hitler turned his attentions to the east, where he was determined to destroy the menace of Soviet communism once and for all, both were to be decisive. Despite the apparent strength and power of the Wehrmacht, displayed to such effect in Poland, Scandinavia and France, it did contain the seeds of its own eventual destruction. The Germans had not got it completely right.

Left: With the Eiffel Tower in the background, the Nazi flag is flown for the first time over occupied Paris, June 1940. The campaign to defeat the French had been short, sharp and decisive, leading to political and military collapse – the epitome of blitzkrieg. Paris would not be liberated until August 1944.

Right: German staff officers, belonging to the headquarters of Field Marshal Gerd von Rundstedt's Army Group, tour the Maginot Line, 1940. Designed to create a barrier to a German attack, the Maginot Line was rendered useless once it had been outflanked.

CHAPTER 3
BALKAN INTERLUDE

The conquest of Yugoslavia, Greece and Crete in the spring of 1941 was an awesome demonstration of German armed might, however it also delayed the start of Operation Barbarossa, the Wehrmacht's invasion of Russia.

Left: An Unteroffizier fires a Leuchtpistole flare pistol to signal the start of an attack in Mostar, Bosnia, April 1941.

Above: General Ewald von Kleist (right), commander of the First Panzer Army in Yugoslavia, at a checkpoint, May 1941.

The German seizure of Western Europe changed the strategic landscape. Throughout its short history, the unified state of Germany had faced the nightmare of a war on two fronts simultaneously, one in the west against France and its allies, the other in the east against Russia. Hitler, from his knowledge of the Great War, was aware of this and, once the ideological differences between National Socialism and Communism had been added to the equation, making a clash in the east virtually inevitable, knew he had to ensure that his western flank was secure before turning on the Soviet Union. Skilful diplomacy (and the offer of land in eastern Poland, an offer that was readily accepted) had kept Soviet leader Joseph Stalin quiet during late 1939 and early 1940, allowing the Wehrmacht to be concentrated against the western

allies, but if communism was to be rooted out at source by military means as Hitler intended, elaborate preparations would need to be made. As early as 1 August 1940, the Führer (in Directive No 17) ordered that the army should be increased to 180 field divisions and that the projected invasion of Britain (Operation Sealion) should be made dependent on naval and air success as preliminaries to an amphibious attack. He was already turning his attentions eastwards.

This was, in hindsight, premature. Despite the heavy losses incurred by Britain during the Battle of France, the British mainland was still secure and could, in the future, be used as a jumping-off point for a re-invasion of the continent. Clearly, this threat would take time to materialize, and Hitler no doubt believed that

Above: *As two Pz Kpfw IV tanks wait in the background, German motorcycle troops negotiate difficult terrain, northern Yugoslavia, April 1941. The motorcycle itself is a BMW R750.*

Right: *A column of Pz Kpfw IIIs enters a typical village on the border between Bulgaria and Greece, April 1941. The tanks are prepared for combat, as shown by the spare track and wheels carried.*

his policy of short, decisive campaigns would also apply to any offensive against the Soviet Union, but the failure to eliminate Britain in the summer of 1940 was a mistake. Furthermore, if Britain had been defeated or politically negated, campaigns in the Balkans and North Africa would have been unnecessary, thus allowing a complete concentration of resources against the Soviet Union when this could have achieved most – during the early stages of any attack.

New weapons and equipment

None of this seemed to matter in the euphoria of 1940, for the Wehrmacht was at the height of its reputation. It had yet to suffer setbacks in battle, let alone defeats, and its combination of panzer divisions, air support and mobility had introduced a new and stunning capability to the art of war. At the same time, its equipment had steadily improved. The Panzer Mark III, a medium tank with enhanced armour and armament, had been made available for the campaigns of 1939 and 1940, and the Mark IV, regarded by many as among the best medium tanks of the Second World War, had made its debut during the attack on France. Improvements to infantry mechanization were displayed as the panzergrenadiers (the infantry attached to panzer divisions) received Schutzenpanzerwagen (Sd Kfz) half-tracks, capable of crossing rough terrain in company with the tanks. In addition, the realization that the 88mm anti-aircraft gun could just as easily be used in the anti-tank role had had a dramatic impact – as Allied tankmen were to find throughout the war, there was little that could withstand such a weapon. Hitler's preference for short campaigns did

Above: A German column, comprising a mix of motorcycles, reconnaissance cars and a Pz Kpfw III, advance unmolested through lightly wooded country in Yugoslavia, April 1941. Note the black cross on the rear of the tank – a recognition symbol that replaced the all-white cross used in the Polish Campaign.

Below: A schwere Zugkraftwagen (sZg Kfz) 18 heavy artillery tractor is used as a recovery vehicle on the narrow roads of central Yugoslavia, April 1941. The trailer it is towing carries the remains of a Pz Kpfw IV Ausf G, damaged by what would appear to be an anti-tank mine which has destroyed a track.

mean that German industry was not yet geared up to providing weapons in abundance, and casualties suffered by the Wehrmacht in Poland, Scandinavia and Western Europe were already putting strain on the manpower source, but there was little reason to doubt German military superiority at this stage.

Nevertheless, the expansion to the army ordered by Hitler on 1 August 1940 was not easy to put into effect. Ten of the new divisions were to be armoured, doubling the apparent size of the panzer arm, but in the event this could only be achieved by splitting existing formations. Each of the 10 divisions that had taken part in the French campaign lost one of its two panzer regiments, reducing the tank establishment of a division to about 140, and

received an extra rifle regiment of motorized (or, in some cases, truck-borne) infantry in compensation. In short, no additional tanks were deployed despite the increase in the number of divisions (though the number of armoured divisions had increased from 15 in May 1940 to 32 in June 1941, the number of tanks rose by only just under a third, from 2574 to 3332). A similar policy was applied to the infantry, where experienced regiments were extracted from existing divisions to act as the core of new formations, being replaced (if at all) by new recruits. This meant, in effect, that the Wehrmacht did not improve its fighting efficiency, despite its eventual increase by June 1941 to 205 divisions, 65 more than it had fielded a year previously. In addition, little was

Right: German motorcycle troops escort a column of Leichter Panzerspahwagen (Sd Kfz) 221 armoured cars during the advance into Greece, April 1941. At this stage of the war the Sd Kfz 221 was armed with a single machine gun mounted in the turret.

Left: German gunners prepare to fire their 75mm Panzerabwehrkanone 40 in rocky terrain in Yugoslavia. The Pak 40, designed in 1939, did not enter service until late 1941, so this photograph was probably taken during an anti-partisan sweep in 1942 or 1943. Note the size of the shell.

done to improve the logistic support needed by these formations, the vast majority of which remained dependent on horse-drawn transport. These weaknesses, disguised by the victories of 1940, were to become obvious once the Wehrmacht was committed to the vast open spaces of the Soviet Union.

Tentative planning for what would become known as Operation Barbarossa (the invasion of Russia) began in the late summer of 1940, and troop movements from west to east became apparent at much the same time. But other strategic factors muddied the water. The projected invasion of Britain was not postponed until October, when it became obvious that the Luftwaffe had failed to gain the required air superiority over southern England, but it was in the Mediterranean and Balkans that more crucial events occurred. These arose from the fact that Hitler's ally Benito Mussolini, fascist leader of Italy, had declared war on Britain and France on 10 June 1940, intent on gaining easy victories against already weakened powers. Unfortunately for the so-called Axis (Italo-German) alliance, Mussolini's forces had proved incapable of achieving such victories. Despite initial gains in East Africa, where the Italians occupied British Somaliland in July, little

headway was made in Egypt (invaded in September) or Greece (attacked in October); instead, in all three theatres, counter-attacks were soon to lead to Italian withdrawals and German embarrassment. If the British cleared North and East Africa, while sending troops to aid the Greeks, the southern flank of the German empire in Europe would be exposed, just as Hitler was preparing to concentrate his forces for an advance to the east. He had little choice but to send elements of the Wehrmacht to the aid of his ally.

Plans for the Balkan offensive

As far as North Africa was concerned, this involved the deployment of no more than a couple of mobile divisions, with support formations attached (see Chapter 4), but the situation in the Balkans was much more dangerous. Germany depended on Rumania for much of its oil – a commodity that was essential to blitzkrieg – and could not afford to leave its southern flank unprotected. To begin with, the problem was solved by diplomacy – both Rumania and Hungary had joined the Axis alliance by the end of 1940 and German troops had been deployed into both countries with the agreement of local dictators – but as the Greeks

Below: Infantry soldiers, equipped with rifles and a machine gun, shelter by the side of a road, possibly in southern Greece, April 1941. Their wary expressions suggest that they are expecting an air attack, although the tank in the background appears to be making no effort to escape.

Above: Mechanics work on a Sturmgeschutz (StuG) III assault gun, taking advantage of the shade offered by a grove of trees in southern Greece, 1941. The StuG III was based on the Pz Kpfw III chassis, with a long-barrelled 75mm gun and 3in (80mm) of armour protection, and was used for infantry support.

counter-attacked and drove the Italian invaders back into Albania, it was obvious that the crisis was by no means over. As early as 18 November 1940 Hitler, therefore, ordered planning to take place for a short, decisive offensive into the Balkans, aimed at ensuring that Yugoslavia, Bulgaria and, to a lesser extent, Turkey accepted Germany hegemony and backed the destruction of Greece. The campaign would have to be short if troops were to be ready for the projected invasion of Russia, set for the late spring of 1941. In the event, Bulgaria agreed to the stationing of Wehrmacht units on its soil and Turkey remained quiet, but political crises in Yugoslavia in early 1941 meant that diplomatic attempts to bring that country into the Axis fold failed. By April, Adolf Hitler had to accept that the campaign would involve invasions of both Yugoslavia and Greece.

The attack on Yugoslavia and Greece

Responsibility for the invasion of Greece lay with the German Twelfth Army (Field Marshal Wilhelm List), concentrated for the purpose in Bulgaria and comprising a total of 12 divisions. On 27 March 1941, Hitler made the decision to include Yugoslavia in the attack, so when the invasion began on 6 April, XL Panzer Corps had to be diverted westwards to Skopje, leaving the incursion into Greece to be carried out initially by XVIII Corps alone. Other units deployed to attack Yugoslavia included Second Army (Weichs) which advanced south from Austria and Hungary and XLI Motorized Corps which attacked toward Belgrade from Rumania.

As it happened, Yugoslavian resistance was weak, enabling XL Panzer Corps to occupy Skopje and then move south towards the Monastir area of northern Greece. This proved to be a decisive

move, introducing forces behind the main Anglo-Greek lines and threatening to cut off Greek forces in Albania. Meanwhile, XVIII Corps had successfully outflanked the Aliakhmon Line in Macedonia and, by 9 April, was marching into Salonika, forcing the Allies back. Three days later, the British withdrew to positions around Mount Olympus and then, when that was threatened with outflanking by fast-moving German columns, to the Thermopylae Line, defending the approaches to Athens. By 20 April, with Yugoslavia collapsing and Greek forces in disarray, the British made the decision to evacuate their remaining units by sea, leaving Germany in possession of Greece. It had been a remarkably swift campaign, even by the familiar standards of blitzkrieg (factors that had contributed to the German victory included the failure of the defenders to exploit the advantages of the mountainous terrain, and the Greeks' failure to support the British Expeditionary Force).

But the offensive was not yet over, for Hitler had also targeted the island of Crete, the capture of which would allow Axis forces to dominate the Aegean Sea and, by implication, deny the British the opportunity to counter-attack from North Africa. This was known to the British, who were intercepting and decrypting German Enigma code messages, and the island appeared to be adequately defended. About 27,000 of the troops evacuated from

Greece had been sent to Crete, where they joined an existing garrison of 3000 British and up to 14,000 Greek soldiers. However, the defenders lacked air support, something that would prove to be crucial when the German plan for invasion emerged. Although some elements of the Wehrmacht would be landed from the sea, their arrival was to be presaged by airborne landings in the first (and, as it turned out, only) attempt to achieve strategic results using parachute and gliderborne units.

About 15,000 German airborne troops of XI Flieger Corps under Major General Kurt Student were ordered to land along the northern coast of the island. As soon as they had secured airfields at Máleme, Canea and Heráklion, men of the 5th Mountain Division would be flown in by Junkers Ju-52 transports and gliders. The rest of the division would then arrive by sea to consolidate and clear the interior. The attack, code-named Operation Merkur, began early on 20 May and did not go well. Around

Right: *Field Marshal List pays an official visit to mountain troops in Greece, 1941, where he is seen talking to three junior non-commissioned officers. The Gefreiter in the centre has been awarded the Iron Cross First Class (pinned to his tunic) and Second Class (denoted by the ribbon in his buttonhole).*

Below: *Field Marshal Wilhelm List, commander of the Twelfth Army, takes the salute at a victory parade in Athens, 7 May 1941. The troops are in Schutzenpanzerwagen (Sd Kfz) 251 half-tracks. To List's rear is SS-Gruppenführer Josef 'Sepp' Dietrich, implying that the troops are Waffen-SS.*

Above: German paratroopers drop from Junkers Ju-52 transport aircraft, May 1941. The 7th Parachute Division landed in two waves, capturing Máleme airfield after two days of fighting, and thereby securing a base for further reinforcements. Crete was a victory, but the cost in men and aircraft was high.

Left: General von Kleist takes the salute as a Pz Kpfw IV Ausf D of the 11th Panzer Division drives past. The building is the Skupshtina, or Yugoslav Parliament, locating the parade in Belgrade on 14 April 1941. The 11th Panzer Division advanced from Bulgaria to seize the Yugoslav capital.

Máleme, elements of the Sturmregiment landed in the midst of strongly held New Zealand positions and were almost wiped out, while men of the 3rd Regiment quickly became bogged down in 'Prison Valley' to the south of Canea. A second wave of airborne troops fared no better, and it began to seem as if the operation had failed. However, British command confusion led to the abandonment of Hill 107, overlooking Máleme airfield, on 21 May, an event seized upon by Student, who ordered Ju-52s carrying reinforcements to land, despite artillery fire across the runway. This proved to be the turning point, for once Máleme was in German hands, there was little to stop the flow of men and supplies.

British commanders were convinced that the airborne landings were little more than an elaborate feint, preparing the way for the main amphibious assault. Thus when naval transports carrying men of the 5th Mountain Division were intercepted at sea on the night of 21/22 May and dispersed, it was assumed that the threat had receded. This was far from the case. As more German reinforcements arrived by air, British counter-attacks failed to dislodge the Germans from their newly acquired positions, while Student's continued pressure on Canea and Heráklion gradually forced the defenders back. The British garrison at Heráklion was evacuated by sea on 28/29 May, allowing the Germans to open up another aerial lifeline; by then, the broader decision had been made to pull as many of the Anglo-Greek units as possible off the island. By 1 June, Crete was firmly in German hands.

Victory on Crete

It was a hard-fought victory for the airborne troops, and their losses had been severe – 6500 men killed or wounded and, significantly, over 40 Ju-52s destroyed – but it did mean that the Balkan region had been secured before Operation Barbarossa, scheduled for 22 June, began. Hitler was never to use the airborne units again for independent operations, something that was to have profound effects on the Axis plans for the seizure of Malta (arguably a more important strategic objective than Crete), but Student's men had added to the growing reputation of the Wehrmacht as a fighting force. That was about to change in the nightmare of the Eastern Front.

THE ARMY IN AFRICA

From the beginning of 1941 the Wehrmacht became involved in Italy's war in North Africa. The German commander, Erwin Rommel, was a master tactician on the battlefield who nearly secured a German strategic victory.

Left: General Erwin Rommel (1891-1944) with two of his commanders – one German and one Italian.

Above: Staff officers cluster around a schwerer Panzerspahwagen Sd Kfz 232 armoured car, North Africa, 1941.

German diversions to save their Italian allies were not confined to the Balkans. Mussolini's invasion of Egypt, initiated in September 1940, soon bogged down and, when the British Western Desert Force, commanded by Major General Richard O'Connor, counter-attacked in early December, the Italians suddenly found themselves out-manoeuvred and out-fought. By 7 February 1941, over 130,000 Italians had surrendered to O'Connor's men and the British had taken possession of the whole of Cyrenaica, the eastern half of the Italian colony of Libya, plus 400 tanks and over 800 guns. British casualties amounted to less than 2000. With concurrent victories in East Africa, the British seemed on the verge of destroying Mussolini's empire.

If this had occurred and the British had been allowed to advance further west, towards the key port of Tripoli, any chances of reversing the situation by pouring in reinforcements from southern Europe would have been dashed. In the event, Mussolini

Above: Rommel (centre) emerges from a planning conference held in his headquarters at Benghazi, Libya, early 1942. In the shadow of the doorway the bulky figure of Field Marshal Albrecht Kesselring (1885-1960) may be seen.

Right: German troops mop up in Benghazi after recapturing the port in early April 1941. The truck on the left, which appears to contain British prisoners of war, is typical of the vehicles that were essential to the resupply of both sides' forces in North Africa.

survived for two interconnected reasons. First, General Sir Archibald Wavell, British Commander-in-Chief Middle East, was ordered by Prime Minister Winston Churchill to halt the advance and divert troops to Greece, already under threat from Axis attack. Secondly, Mussolini appealed to Hitler for aid and the Führer, somewhat reluctantly, agreed to send elements of the Wehrmacht to North Africa.

Rommel's first offensive

On 12 February 1941, less than a week after the Italian defeat, Lieutenant General Erwin Rommel, erstwhile commander of the 7th Panzer Division, arrived in Tripoli with lead troops of what would shortly be entitled the Deutsches Afrika Korps. The force was not large – initially no more than two divisions, the 15th Panzer and 5th Light – but its impact was felt immediately. Without waiting for all his troops to arrive, Rommel went onto the offensive, pushing the over-stretched and under-strength British back from positions around el Agheila as far as the Egyptian border. Tobruk held out, defying Rommel's repeated efforts to take it,

Below: *A Pak 38 anti-tank gun is positioned in desert terrain, 1941. The photograph clearly indicates the problems of fighting in North Africa – the desert is wide open, and even after having scraped out a position, the gun-crew is still exposed. Dress of the soldiers shows adaptation to desert conditions.*

Above: *The crew of a 50mm Panzerabwehrkanone (Pak) 38 anti-tank gun occupy a position on a sand-ridge, waiting for the enemy to appear. The photograph was probably taken in early 1941, before many Afrika Korps soldiers had dispensed with the pith helmet in favour of the more comfortable service cap.*

but in all other respects, by early May 1941 the British were back where they had started.

In mid-May and again a month later, the British tried to advance, only to be held along the Libyan-Egyptian border, but when they repeated the process in November 1941 in Operation Crusader, they not only managed to relieve Tobruk but also, after exceptionally heavy fighting, forced Rommel back to el Agheila. However, he quickly bounced back, advancing to positions south of Gazala in January 1942, where British and Free French defences precluded further progress.

Rommel built up his strength there and, in May 1942, out-flanked the Gazala Line, taking Tobruk and pushing the Allies back across the Egyptian border towards defences hastily established around el Alamein. Attacks in July (the First Battle of

Above: A 20mm Flugabwehrkanone (Flak) 30 light anti-aircraft gun operating in the ground role, North Africa, 1941. The Flak 30, accepted as standard issue by the Wehrmacht in 1935, proved particularly useful at laying down rapid fire – about 120 rounds a minute – at ground targets.

Alamein) and late August (Alam Halfa) failed to achieve a break-through, allowing General Sir Bernard Montgomery, newly appointed commander of the British Eighth Army, to prepare his own offensive. When this began in late October 1942 (the Second Battle of Alamein), Rommel was forced back, this time all the way to Tunisia, where Anglo-US armies, landed in French North Africa in November, were pushing eastwards. Even then, the Axis forces held on, not surrendering until Tunis itself was taken in May 1943.

Left: *Rommel views the enemy through a powerful set of binoculars while a soldier behind him plots his exact position by means of a sun compass. In the desert, accurate positioning was essential, although this did not stop even experienced soldiers getting lost.*

Below: *Rommel's command caravan during the North African campaign – an AEC Mark II armoured truck captured from the British. The vehicle has large recognition symbols painted on front and sides to avoid clashes with friendly forces, and is marked with the emblem of 21st Panzer Division.*

In short, the North African campaign between 1940 and 1943 consisted essentially of a see-saw.

The reasons for this were varied. As a theatre of war, North Africa had a number of characteristics that made it suited to mobile, wide-ranging operations. It contained no substantial urban areas – the only permanent settlements were along the thin coastal fringe – and little indigenous population, allowing the rival armies to choose their avenues of advance with a fair degree of freedom. At the same time, within the parameters of the coast and the soft-sand desert to the south, the going was reasonably firm, permitting armoured forces to build up unprecedented momen-

tum, at least in western Egypt and Cyrenaica. To many who fought there, North Africa seemed to be uniquely suited to armoured engagements.

But it was also a quartermaster's nightmare. Both sides were dependent for their supplies of fuel, equipment, ammunition, manpower and food on outside sources, access to which spelt the difference between success and failure in battle. The British, in possession of the Nile Delta, enjoyed some advantages, but even they had to ship supplies through the Mediterranean (a dangerous enterprise for much of the campaign) or, as an alternative, all the way round Africa, via the Cape, into the Red Sea. By comparison,

Right: As Axis forces move towards the perimeter, Tobruk comes under heavy air and artillery bombardment, June 1942. Defended principally by ill-prepared South African troops of the 2nd South African Division, the Tobruk fortifications had been largely dismantled since December 1941, leaving the port very vulnerable to assault. Its loss was a major blow to Allied morale.

Below: An Italian resupply column snakes its way through the Sollum Pass on the border between Libya and Egypt, June 1942. Abandoned British equipment lines the road, indicating the haste with which the Eighth Army had retreated from Gazala. The vulnerability of truck convoys to air attack can be readily appreciated.

Above: A German soldier walks through the main square in Tobruk shortly after the capture of the port in June 1942. Besieged by Rommel between April and December 1941, Tobruk had been relieved by the British in Operation Crusader, only to fall to Axis forces after the Allied defeat at Gazala.

Rommel's supply lines were far shorter – from southern Italy to Tripoli – although they were also very vulnerable to interdiction. As long as the British retained possession of Malta, Axis convoys were subject to air, naval and submarine attacks that could gravely restrict Rommel's ability to fight. Equally importantly, even if sufficient supplies were delivered to North Africa, both sides faced the additional problem of moving them to their front-line forces. Only the coastal road was capable of sustaining heavy traffic, and trucks rarely ventured into areas that might contain soft sand or rocks. If they did, the wear and tear on suspensions, gearboxes and clutch plates often meant that they broke down, placing more pressure on resupply not only because one less truck meant one less load, but also because vehicle spares would need to be found and delivered. It was a vicious circle.

Above: The scourge of British armour in the desert: an 88mm Flugabwehrkanone (Flak) 18, used in the ground role. This particular example is mounted on a Sonderhanger 201 trailer for towing behind an eight-ton Zugkraftwagen Sd Kfz 7. No Allied tanks could withstand a hit from an '88'.

This, more than anything else, gave the North African campaign its see-saw character. Success for the British meant that they advanced away from their supply bases in Egypt, stretching the capability of vehicle convoys to keep up; success for Rommel had the same effect by pulling him away from his supply base at Tripoli. Thus, advances of 300-450 miles (500-700km) might occur, but the victors would inevitably become over-stretched and vulnerable. At the first sign of enemy counter moves, the lead elements of the advancing force would snap back as if on a piece of elastic, withdrawing on their own supply lines with often unseemly alacrity. Once secure again, they too could counterattack, precipitating an enemy retreat.

In the end, the British largely solved this problem by building up massive stockpiles of vehicles and supplies before attacking at Second Alamein, but Rommel never enjoyed that luxury. With the war on the Eastern Front raging by the late summer of 1941, the Afrika Korps was low down the list of Hitler's priorities for supplies, and the 'Desert Fox' was forced to fight on a shoestring,

Above: A battery of German artillery – schwere 100mm Kanone 18 guns – prepares to lay down a bombardment onto Allied positions, 1942. The terrain suggests that the Axis forces have left the sand-desert behind and are now occupying positions in western Libya or eastern Tunisia.

Right: A mixed army and paratrooper patrol, supported by a Pz Kpfw II light tank, probes forward into a small village in Tunisia, 1943. The paratroopers, in their distinctive rimless helmets and smocks, are Luftwaffe personnel, but they are fighting alongside the army as infantry.

often surviving only because he captured enemy fuel and food dumps (as, for example, at Tobruk in June 1942). In addition, the British made it a deliberate policy to target Axis supply ships as they moved towards Tripoli, concentrating particularly on oil tankers to starve Rommel's panzers of vital fuel. Air strikes against road convoys from Tripoli to the frontline were also favoured, although they did depend on Allied air superiority and access to airbases within range.

British tactics in North Africa

Such problems make Rommel's record in North Africa all the more remarkable, for there is no doubt that between March 1941 and at least October 1942 he consistently outfought his British enemies, even though they often had superior numbers and adequate equipment. To a certain extent, this was the fault of British commanders who, once O'Connor had been captured in April 1941, lacked the flair or imagination to conduct blitzkrieg-style offensives. This was shown in the abortive attacks on the Libyan-Egyptian border in May-June 1941, and on the Gazala Line a year later, when plodding, predictable and uncoordinated advances left them vulnerable to defeat. Indeed, even when the British did achieve victory, as in Operation Crusader in November-December 1941 and at Alamein in 1942, they depended largely on overwhelming numbers and massed firepower to shatter their enemy before advancing relatively slowly to take ground. Rommel, by comparison, was a past master at mobile warfare, targeting his

enemies rather than the land they temporarily occupied, aiming to destroy their cohesion as much as their military hardware.

His favourite tactical ploy was to use the open southern flank of the desert, to conduct sweeping moves designed to come up behind enemy fixed defences and sever the links between front-line 'muscle' and its command 'brain'. This was a characteristic of Rommel's first offensive in March 1941, when panzers suddenly appeared to catch weary British units unawares, but it reached its apogee at Gazala in May 1942. On that occasion, faced with a series of British defended 'boxes' from the coast down to the Free French fortress at Bir Hacheim, Rommel used Italian and German

Above: General Jurgen von Arnim (1891-1971), commander of Armee Gruppe Afrika in Tunisia after Rommel's departure in March 1943, shakes hands with one of his soldiers while on an inspection tour of front-line positions. Von Arnim was captured by the Allies in May 1943, when the Tunisian campaign ended.

infantry to fix the defenders in place while concentrating his armour for a sweep south.

The plan was to skirt round Bir Hacheim before advancing north, behind the Allied defences, so unhinging the Gazala Line. It did not go as smoothly as Rommel would have liked; the Free

French held out, creating a rock in the path of the panzer advance, and some of the 'boxes' were more strongly defended than anticipated. By 28 May, two days after the start of the attack, Rommel was effectively trapped between British defences and his own minefields in an area dubbed 'the Cauldron', but his dynamic style of leadership, coupled to a lamentable lack of coordination on the British side, allowed him to break out after two weeks of hard fighting. Not only did the British pull back all the way to Alamein, but they also left Tobruk to be seized, along with 2000 serviceable vehicles. It was Rommel's finest hour, and Hitler made him a field marshal as a reward.

Alam Halfa and Second Alamein

Such stunning successes, often against all the odds, spread Rommel's reputation far and wide – one of Montgomery's first acts as commander of Eighth Army in August 1942 was to remind his troops that the 'Desert Fox' was not infallible – and ensured him the undying loyalty of his men. To have served in the Afrika Korps was (and still is) regarded as having fought in a 'clean' campaign, unsullied by the atrocities of the Eastern Front, and although Rommel enjoyed less support from the Italians, many of whom,

Below: A well camouflaged 75mm Panzerabwehrkanone (Pak) 40 anti-tank gun awaits the arrival of Allied armour on the approaches to Tunis, April 1943. With mountains and trees in the background, it may be appreciated that the terrain has changed from the open deserts of Cyrenaica and Egypt.

being foot-or truck-borne, tended to be left behind when he pulled back, the members of the Wehrmacht who served in North Africa prided themselves on their achievements. The desert may have had its problems – heat, flies and desert sores could make life miserable at times – but it was better than freezing on the steppes of Russia or dying in the ruins of Stalingrad.

But even Rommel could not achieve the final victory. He came within 60 miles (95km) of Alexandria in July 1942 but, in Montgomery, the British had found a general who was prepared to counter his enemy's advantages. Denying Rommel mobility at Alam Halfa, Montgomery built up his strength to such an extent that when he finally attacked in late October, he did so in full knowledge that his enemy was desperately short of fuel and spare parts. In addition, Rommel could not manoeuvre, as before, by moving south into the open desert, for one feature of the Alamein Line was that it rested on the Qattara Depression, an area of broken terrain that was, indeed, impassable. Montgomery may not have conducted the sort of flowing operations associated with blitzkrieg, but he was astute enough to realize that Rommel's style of command was not best suited to positional warfare. By imposing an attritional battle on the Afrika Korps, the Eighth Army made the most of its natural strengths and directed them firmly at Rommel's weaknesses. The simultaneous landings in Northwest Africa of over 100,000 British and American troops (Operation Torch, initiated on 8 November 1942) merely made Rommel's dilemma much worse, for he now faced the prospect of attacks from both west and east. The fact that he conducted a masterly

Right: A 37mm Flak 36, mounted on the back of a Zugkraftwagen Sd Kfz 7/2, guards the harbour at Tunis against Allied air attack, 1942. The shipping in the harbour, representing a major lifeline with Europe, shows how vulnerable the port was. The lack of damage implies bombing has yet to begin.

Left: A column of Sturmgeschutz IV assault guns drives through the Italian port of Naples en route to Tunisia, 1943. The StuG IV, built on the chassis of a Pz Kpfw IV, was fitted with an effective 75mm main gun and protected by more than 6in (152mm) of concrete on top of the normal steel armour.

Below: Members of the Afrika Korps sort out their equipment, having arrived at Tunis airport aboard the Junkers Ju-52/3m transport aircraft in the background. It was from this airport, that selected personnel were evacuated to Sicily in the final days of the Tunisian campaign.

withdrawal from Alamein to Tunisia, where he linked up with Wehrmacht units hastily committed by Hitler to oppose Operation Torch, does not alter the reality of his eventual defeat.

The end of the Afrika Korps

Rommel did not witness the final surrender in Tunis. In the aftermath of a successful foray against inexperienced American units in the Kasserine Pass in February 1943 – where the American II Corps lost 300 killed, 3000 wounded and 3000 missing, mostly captured – he was invalided back to Germany, suffering from exhaustion. Hitler promoted and fêted him, aware of the popular appeal of the 'Desert Fox', but this can have been small consolation to those who had served under him in North Africa. As the remnants of the Afrika Korps marched into captivity in May, having participated in the tough mountain fighting that characterized the Tunisian campaign, Germany lost one of its most experienced and battle-hardened formations.

CHAPTER 5
OPERATION BARBAROSSA

On 22 June 1941, Hitler began the greatest land war in recorded history. But the invasion of the Soviet Union, launched with such high expectations, would soon turn into a nightmare for millions of German soldiers.

Left: General Heinz Guderian (1888-1954). In June 1941 he led the Second Panzer Group in Russia, part of Army Group Centre.

Above: An infantry section crosses the River Bug at a point dividing German and Soviet occupation zones in Poland.

H itler issued his directive for Operation Barbarossa – the invasion of the Soviet Union – on 18 December 1940. Army Group North (Field Marshal Ritter von Leeb), comprising three panzer, two motorized and twenty-four infantry divisions, was to advance out of East Prussia to take the Baltic states of Lithuania, Latvia and Estonia, before linking up with Finnish troops around Leningrad. Army Group Centre (Field Marshal Fedor von Bock), comprising one cavalry, nine panzer, six motorized and

thirty-three infantry divisions, was to attack eastwards towards Moscow, but halt once it had taken Smolensk and await further orders. Army Group South (Field Marshal Gerd von Rundstedt), comprising five panzer, three motorized and thirty-four infantry divisions, plus Rumanian formations, was to push into the Ukraine, aiming for Rostov.

Barbarossa was an enormous undertaking, involving three million soldiers, 600,000 vehicles, 3580 tanks in 17 panzer divisions

Right: With the strain of battle beginning to show, an infantry machine-gun team, equipped with an MG 34, prepares for the next move into the Soviet Union, late June 1941. By this time, the panzers have moved far ahead, leaving a dangerously exposed gap between themselves and their supporting infantry.

Below: A German soldier orders Soviet prisoners of war out of their crude shelter, 22 June 1941. The chances of survival for these prisoners are slim: if they are suspected of being political commissars, they are likely to be shot; if ordinary soldiers, they face a future of forced labour.

and 7184 artillery pieces, backed by a Luftwaffe of 1830 aircraft. The startline stretched for over 1500km (nearly 1000 miles), from the Baltic to the Black Sea; the advances were to be up to 1100km (700 miles) in depth and the operation was not to begin until 22 June 1941, leaving less than four months before the notorious autumn rains set in.

The Red Army prior to Barbarossa

Despite the ideological differences that existed between Germany and the Soviet Union – differences that made some sort of armed clash inevitable – Stalin was caught by surprise on 22 June. Lulled into a false sense of security by the Non-Aggression Pact he had signed with Hitler in August 1939, and obsessed with internal problems, he had made few specific preparations for war. The 'Red Army of Workers and Peasants' was immensely strong on paper – by 1941 the main Field Army, most of which was packed along the border areas, comprised 151 infantry divisions, 32 cavalry divisions and 38 mechanized brigades, equipped with more than 12,000 armoured fighting vehicles – but it had been significantly weakened by a series of politically-inspired purges in the late 1930s. These had deprived the army of much of its higher command and left its surviving officers afraid to show initiative for fear of Stalin's wrath; in addition, the ordinary soldiers were not well trained or highly motivated. The Red Army was, in many ways, more vulnerable to a blitzkrieg-style assault designed to undermine cohesion than to a conventional attritional campaign.

For these reasons, the initial German attacks enjoyed stunning success. In the north, General Erich Hoepner's 4th Panzer Group

Below: As a village burns, German infantry race forward to consolidate new positions, making sure that the enemy has no chance to recover from the shock of the Barbarossa attack. This photograph, taken in June 1941 near Brest-Litovsk, shows soldiers attached to Guderian's Second Panzer Group.

Above: An infantry group, commanded by the Feldwebel (Company Sergeant Major) standing in the centre, moves cautiously through agricultural terrain in the Ukraine, summer 1941. Most of the soldiers have extemporized fittings for camouflage branches to their helmets.

Above: *A machine-gun section moves to new positions in a Russian village, autumn 1941. The barn may not have been set ablaze by the advancing Germans, for it was a deliberate Soviet ploy, ordered by Stalin, to leave nothing of value to the invading enemy. The order would soon pay dividends.*

Right: *German infantry enter Minsk, early July 1941. The lack of damage to buildings indicates that little fighting has taken place; indeed, with the panzers having already surrounded the city, it is now an isolated pocket, waiting to be mopped up. But the soldiers still face urban battle.*

reached Daugavpils and crossed the River Dvina as early as 26 June; by 14 July his lead tanks were within 80 miles of Leningrad. Further south, panzers of General Hermann Hoth's 3rd and General Heinz Guderian's 2nd Panzer Groups conducted a series of massive envelopments, (Guderian advanced 270 miles (434km) in the first seven days of the offensive) surrounding the Soviet Tenth Army and closing on Minsk by 29 June. Altogether, these advances yielded over 200,000 demoralized Soviet prisoners. By 16 July, Guderian had even taken Smolensk and seemed poised to strike for Moscow. In the far south, von Rundstedt's formations had advanced deep into the Ukraine.

But problems were already building up. The speed of the panzer advances, together with their destruction of existing road systems, left the infantry divisions lagging far behind (by late July,

Guderian estimated that his supporting infantry were up to two weeks' marching time to his rear), while the need to round up the vast numbers of prisoners and consolidate territorial gains merely made the situation worse.

Supply and terrain problems

More significantly, the supply chains needed to keep the armies moving proved virtually impossible to set up. The Soviet road system was rudimentary and soon collapsed entirely; the railway was a broader gauge than that of the rest of Europe, necessitating either trans-shipment of supplies at the border or a complete reconstruction of the system; and Stalin's declared policy of 'scorched earth' denied anything of value to the invaders.

Nor did the nature of the terrain aid the Germans: in the north,

Right: The reality of summer campaigning in southern Russia, 1941: a German infantry column, led by a twin-mounted anti-aircraft MG 34 in the back of a horse-drawn cart (known as an MG Doppelwagen), shows the strain. The broiling heat has led many to cover their heads with makeshift covers.

Left: Two 37mm Panzerabwehrkanone (Pak) 35/36 anti-tank guns cover the advance of infantry through a town in western Russia, 1941. The fact that the guns are exposed and the crews fairly relaxed, implies that little opposition is expected. Note the boxes of 37mm ammunition leaning against the wall.

von Leeb's men found themselves slowed by the large forests of the Baltic states; Army Groups Centre and South were split by the impassable Pripet Marshes; in the south, von Rundstedt's units faced the enormity of the Steppes. Finally, despite the collapse of vast portions of the Red Army under the initial onslaught, parts of it did hold out, not least the Fifth Army on the southern fringes of the Pripet Marshes, where they not only used the terrain to advantage but also surprised the Germans by fielding the new T-34 tank, equipped with sloped armour and an effective 76mm gun, which could more than hold its own with any German tank in operation at that time.

Above: Motorcycle reconnaissance troops pause for a hasty meal, taking advantage of lightly wooded terrain to shelter. The cross in a circle, marked on the mudguard of the BMW R-12 motorcycle, shows that these are soldiers of the 3rd Panzer Division, part of Army Group Centre in Operation Barbarossa.

As each problem emerged, delays were imposed on the German advance, allowing Stalin time to recover his balance. At the same time, the controversies over strategy came to a head. The generals of OKH were still pressing for a concentrated thrust

Right: *Panzergrenadiers, having arrived in a well built village in their half-track, round up two Soviet prisoners, neither of whom seems to be particularly concerned about his plight. Purporting to have been taken during Operation Barbarossa, this photograph may be no more than a propaganda shot, designed for domestic consumption.*

Below: *German infantry soldiers hitch a ride during the advance on Moscow in the summer of 1941. The roadway is still covered in dust, but it will not be long before the autumn rains turn it to mud. The vehicle is equipped to lay field telephones – a vital function in any advance.*

Left: *With an MG 34 on his shoulder and a belt of 7.92mm ammunition at the ready, a machine-gunner takes part in the advance on Moscow, 1941. The photograph was taken as the autumn weather closes in – the soldier has donned both greatcoat and gloves – but far worse is to come.*

Top right: *Something catches the attention of infantrymen using a Leichter Schutzenpanzerwagen (Sd Kfz) 250 half-track as a radio command post. The soldier seated on the right has a 9mm Maschinenpistole 40 submachine gun (widely, but erroneously, called the Schmeisser) across his knees. Note also the MG 34 for anti-aircraft use.*

Bottom right: *German infantry attend a briefing as they enter a town in the Ukraine, summer 1941. By now, these men have marched more than 200 miles (323km) since the opening of Operation Barbarossa, and the strain is beginning to tell. They are clearly exhausted and have had little opportunity to rest.*

Above: *As evening approaches, an infantry squad sets up a defensive position, centred around their MG 34 machine gun, shown here on a tripod mount for sustained, long-range firing. The photograph was taken in Kiev in September 1941. The preparations for attack suggest stiffening Soviet resistance.*

Below: *German troops advance into a shattered Russian town, autumn 1941. Their greatcoats imply that the weather is deteriorating. The fact that they are bunched together, with no apparent flank guard to clear the houses, suggests that they are either inexperienced or not expecting tough opposition.*

against Moscow, now tantalizingly close, but Hitler was still insistent on destroying the Soviet Field Army. On 19 July, he issued a new directive which altered the entire course of the campaign. The attack in the centre was to be left to the infantry alone once Smolensk had been cleared, with Hoth's panzers diverting north to assist in the seizure of Leningrad and Guderian's moving south to skirt the Pripet Marshes and link up with von Rundstedt around the city of Kiev.

Such a dramatic change took time to put into effect; the next stage of the advance did not begin until 25 August. By then, the reasons for the shift had largely disappeared – in the north, German units had approached Leningrad without the benefit of Hoth's panzers, while Army Group South achieved a breakthrough as early as 3 August – but the Wehrmacht had to obey the Führer's orders. In the event, the advance by Guderian's troops was spectacular, encountering little opposition and making contact with von Rundstedt on 16 September at Likhvitsa, 190km (120 miles) to the east of Kiev. The pocket so created yielded another 210,000 Soviet prisoners and opened the way for an advance east towards the Sea of Azov and into the Crimea.

Operation Typhoon begins

By then, Hitler had changed his mind yet again. As early as 6 September, he issued another directive, this time ordering a resumption of the advance on Moscow, with Hoth and Guderian moving back towards their original objective from north and south

Below: A 2 cm Flugabwehrkanone (Flak) 30 light anti-aircraft gun, mounted on a Krupp Protz Kfz 69 six-wheeled truck, is used to lay down ground fire in support of an advance into Odessa, 1941. Note the Sturmgeschutz (StuG) III in the background, available for heavier support fire should it be needed.

Above: *Elements of Army Group South advance towards the Crimea, summer 1941. In the foreground, infantry are using Czech-designed Pz Kpfw 38(t) light tanks as extemporized carriers, while in the background a Pz Kpfw III is pushing past a Pak 38 anti-tank gun.*

Below: *The crew of a StuG III assault gun replenish ammunition stocks for their 75mm cannon from an army truck, southern Russia 1941. Note the Notek lamp on the left mudguard of the StuG: this was designed to ensure that following vehicles kept a safe distance when driving at night.*

Above: Infantry ride into combat aboard Pz Kpfw IV Ausf E tanks, equipped with short-barrelled 75mm main armament. The metal frame under the barrel of the tank in the foreground is an antenna deflector, designed to bend the radio aerial out of the way of the gun barrel when the turret was traversed.

as soon as they had cleared the opposition in their respective areas. Code-named Operation Taifun (Typhoon), this would be the final push of the campaigning season. With Leningrad under siege in the north and the Ukraine in German hands in the south, the chances of success seemed high.

But it was too late. After three months of bitter fighting, surviving German troops and vehicles were operating under incredible strain, made worse by the stifling heat of summer and the ever-present clouds of dust. The railway system had proved impossible to rebuild quickly – the German planners had made no provision for engineers to construct a railway or to protect the system against the growing threat of partisans – and logistics were failing. Moreover, by late September, when Taifun began, Stalin had concentrated his reserves to protect the approaches to Moscow and had successfully boosted the fighting spirit of his soldiers by appealing to their Russian patriotism rather than their communist ideology. Thus, although the German attacks appeared to go well – by mid-October Orel had been seized and fresh encirclements achieved around Bryansk and Vyazma (producing a further 663,000 prisoners) – it was in fact doomed to failure. Under the command of General Georgi Zhukov, the citizens of Moscow were mobilized to dig anti-tank ditches and trenches, while new formations were moved to protect the capital from their pre-war deployment areas in the eastern USSR. This was enough to slow the German advance and allow the traditional saviour of Russia – 'General Winter' – to enter the equation.

Above: Winter conditions begin to have an impact, November 1941. These infantry soldiers, their uniforms sprinkled with the first snows of winter, are feeling the cold, chiefly because they have been issued with nothing more than normal uniforms. Some have procured earmuffs, others are using scarves.

The weather began to break in late October, when sunshine gave way to rain and turned what remained of the roads into quagmires of glutinous mud. Almost overnight, German troops found themselves bogged down while their Soviet opponents, more used to such conditions, retained a degree of basic mobility. The rate of advance stalled as supplies failed to get through and soldiers spent all their time trying to dig their vehicles out of the mud. The situation improved on 6/7 November, when a sudden frost caused the mud to freeze, but the advantage was short-lived. Guderian managed to advance closer to Moscow from the south, and some of the lead elements of the Wehrmacht even entered the outer suburbs of the city, but as the frosts gave way to snow, Taifun ground to a halt. With temperatures down to minus 40 degrees Celsius (minus 40 Fahrenheit), oil in vehicle engines froze, weapons seized up and many soldiers, still equipped for summer fighting, went down with frostbite, exacerbated by exhaustion after so much hard campaigning. By 5 December, the invaders could go no further.

Zhukov had already recognized that his enemy was close to breaking point. Taking advantage of the arrival of over 30

Above: The advance into Russia in 1941 was, for the vast majority of German soldiers, a hard slog, dependent on horse-drawn transport even in an age of mechanized warfare. This slowed them down considerably. Autumn rains, which began in October, did little to help. It was a miserable time.

Mongolian divisions from Siberia, comprising men used to harsh winter conditions, he planned a counter-attack to the north and south of Moscow, where German salients were vulnerable. As the German attacks stalled, Zhukov made his move. On 5 and 6 December, over half a million Soviet troops attacked along a 600-mile (950-km) front from Leningrad to Kursk, appearing out of the mists of winter to shatter the surprised enemy. German units fell apart and Hitler had no choice but to permit withdrawals into a series of 'hedgehog' defences, some up to 200 miles (325km) to the west of the high-tide of the original advance.

Hitler blamed his generals. As early as 19 December, he sacked the Commander-in-Chief, von Brauchitsch, and took over direct

Right: An abiding memory of Operation Barbarossa for many German soldiers, particularly those in the southern parts of Russia, was one of endless, featureless terrain. Here, a group of infantrymen rest by one of the few trees in their area, before moving on over barren ground. In addition, it is getting colder.

Above: An Eisenbahnpanzerzuge (armoured train). Developed in response to partisan attacks, the EisbPzZug shown here includes, a 7.62 cm gun turret and a 20mm Flak 38 quadruple anti-aircraft gun.

Left: As the winter of 1941 sets in, German soldiers – lacking proper issues of winter clothing – have to extemporize. Here, infantry display snow-camouflage suits made out of bed linen.

Right: As the Soviets recover from the initial shock of Barbarossa, German soldiers face the perils of artillery fire – an area in which the Red Army excelled. One answer was to dig in every time the advance paused.

command himself – a logical extension of the Nazification of the Wehrmacht that had begun in 1934. Five days later, he dismissed Guderian, together with the commanders of Army Groups North and Centre. Thereafter, Hitler was to assume increasing responsibility for events on the Eastern Front, interfering at the operational level, which should have been left to his local commanders. Any chance of using initiative was being undermined, forcing the Wehrmacht to become less flexible in its thinking and more positional in its war-fighting.

Meanwhile, Zhukov had continued his assaults, reacting to pressure from Stalin, although he was never able to repeat the success of the first few days of the counter-attack. As the winter

Above: Led by their officers, a German horse-mounted unit advances over desolate, snow-covered terrain during the exceptionally harsh winter of 1941-42. Horses proved to be adaptable to conditions on the Eastern Front, but even they could not withstand the bitter cold. Many thousands perished (or were eaten).

Above: An armoured column, led by a StuG III assault gun, moves forward through a snow-covered village in Russia, December 1941. The image is picturesque, but the reality is harsh. Note the muffled infantrymen.

Left: German motorcycle messengers brave the cold, Eastern Front, winter 1941. The men have used all available means of keeping warm – blankets, greatcoats, captured Russian balaclavas and mouth guards. Even so, they are clearly freezing.

dragged on, both sides fought to retain existing positions, sometimes resorting to hand-to-hand combat with knives and entrenching tools, and often having to fight in the bitterest conditions imaginable. German soldiers who survived were granted a special medal, known colloquially as the 'Order of the Frozen Meat'. It summed up the nightmare.

Germany faces a new kind of war

The failure of Barbarossa was a turning point for the Wehrmacht and the Third Reich. Gone were the days of speedy advances leading inevitably to victory; instead, German soldiers faced a seemingly endless campaign in unimaginable conditions of ferocity and terror against an enemy whose strength was growing. Losses in the first campaigning season had been horrific – nearly three-quarters of a million casualties (many to frostbite) – and the strain on equipment levels was such that German industry could never hope to keep up. Hitler had, without fully realizing the implications, condemned his armed forces and his country to a

total war, the end result of which could only be complete victory for one side or the other. The experiences on the Eastern Front in 1941 provided ample evidence that Germany was struggling, and although some successes were still to come, the writing was beginning to appear on the wall for those who were astute enough to see it.

In addition, the failure of Barbarossa coincided with a widening of the war to one of global proportions. On 7 December 1941, the Japanese attacked the US Pacific Fleet at Pearl Harbor, and six days later Hitler, in an ill-considered fit of alliance solidarity, formally declared war on the USA, awakening an economic giant whose ability to produce weapons would soon outstrip that of the rest of the world put together. In just over two years, the Wehrmacht may have achieved some significant victories, but the policy of short, sharp campaigns could no longer apply. From now on, it would be a long, hard slog – something the Germans had neither the industrial capacity nor the infinite reserves of manpower to sustain.

CHAPTER 6

THE WAR ON THE EASTERN FRONT

The Wehrmacht was bled white in the vast expanses of the western Soviet Union. Both the terrain and nature of the fighting were unlike anything its soldiers had previously experienced, including the nightmare winter.

Left: This motorcyclist enjoys the benefits of a fur-lined coat, cap and gloves in an effort to keep out the wind and cold.

Above: A German anti-tank gun position in winter conditions, 1942. The gun is a 75mm Panzerabwehrkanone (Pak) 97/38.

For the three million German soldiers who fought on the Eastern Front in 1941-42, the experience was traumatic. Everything about the theatre of war was different to anything they had seen before, while the realization that this was a campaign that was not going to be completed in a matter of weeks meant that they had to alter their entire attitude to the conflict. Gone were the days of short, victorious campaigns, followed by a period of leave or relatively easy occupation duties; each German soldier had now to face the prospect of a long, bitterly-fought battle for survival.

Left: In some areas of the Eastern Front, particularly in winter, the German Army had to revert to age-old methods of movement and resupply. Here, a mule column, led by soldiers belonging to a Mountain Division, brings food and ammunition forward through a snow-covered mountain pass in Russia, 1942.

Right: Members of a Pak 97/38 anti-tank guncrew duck as a Soviet artillery shell explodes quite close to their rather exposed position. The gun has been painted white in an effort to camouflage it in the snow, and the soldiers are wearing winter coveralls, but the gun has clearly been spotted by the enemy.

Right: German engineers send a remotely controlled tracked vehicle, known as a Goliath, towards an unseen obstacle. The Goliath, usually driven by an electric motor, contained a 183lb (83kg) explosive charge in the front compartment and a 6562ft (2000m) cable-drum in the rear. Once in position, it was detonated, clearing a path.

Right: Two members of a panzer crew check ammunition links for their machine guns in winter conditions, 1942. Because of the snow, they are probably checking that the links are clear – if frozen or snow-covered, they might jam the machine guns.

Much of this was a direct result of Hitler's own underestimation of his Soviet enemy. Obsessed with the apparent need to destroy communism as a rival ideology, he was convinced that all he had to do was attack and the 'whole rotten edifice' of the Soviet system would come crashing down. To a certain extent, this was not illogical – Stalin's dictatorship had led to widespread social unrest, particularly in those areas of western Russia that were the primary targets of the Barbarossa assault – but it failed to take into account the tenacity of the ordinary Soviet soldier, his fear of his rulers and his love of Mother Russia. Once Stalin had recognized that his army would fight more effectively because of patriotism rather than political ideology, he was able to tap into a source of virtually infinite strength. If the invading Germans had managed to take Moscow or Leningrad, the situation might have been different, but Hitler was correct in one matter – in the end, the capture of physical locations was less important than destroying the will of the Red Army to continue the fight.

Above: *An infantry section catches up on some much-needed sleep, Russia 1942. The immense distances that infantry had to cover, often on their feet, inevitably imposed strain, and soldiers took every opportunity to rest.*

Left: *An infantry NCO checks the route his section is to take towards the enemy before issuing his orders, southern Russia 1942. His eyes display the experience of the man – this is his second season of campaigning on the Eastern Front.*

Right: *With bayonets fixed to their Mauser Kar 98k rifles, a German patrol checks a Russian house, 1942. It is likely that this photograph was taken during one of the periodic anti-partisan sweeps in the area, rather than at the frontline.*

Hitler's optimism about Barbarossa permeated down to the lowliest of his soldiers in June 1941, with the result that they crossed the border into Soviet-occupied territory convinced that the campaign would be over within a matter of weeks. Almost immediately, however, they entered a new and strange environment. Among the first things that struck most German soldiers was the comparative poverty of the peasants, living in what appeared to be little more than hovels, with few signs of organized agriculture. The situation worsened the further east the army went, but for soldiers brought up in the more sophisticated societies of the

Above: An Unteroffizier finds comfort in his rather elaborate pipe as his section prepares to move into a village in southern Russia, 1942. The unit is part of General Paulus's Sixth Army, advancing towards Stalingrad. It is unlikely that either the NCO or his pipe survived for very long.

Left: An infantry Unteroffizier, armed with a 9mm Maschinenpistole 40 submachine gun, prepares to call his men forward, having checked for enemy presence around the corner of the building, summer 1942.

west, the comparison was strong as soon as they entered enemy lands. Few of them spoke any Russian, so attempts to converse with the people invariably failed, leading to a growing belief that the peasants were not only repressed but also unintelligent, reinforcing the Nazi racial propaganda message that the Slavic peoples in general were Untermenschen (an underclass), fit only for slavery under German masters. This had a number of effects, not least that the inherent anti-communism of some of the people of western Russia (notably the Ukrainians, who had suffered severely under Stalin) was just not recognized, and an opportunity for the Germans to exploit this was lost.

At the same time, the attitude of German soldiers towards both the peasants and captured soldiers tended to be harsh. Under orders from Hitler to seek out and execute all 'Bolshevik Jews', many Wehrmacht units, and even more so their Waffen-SS counterparts, acted in ways that were no different to those of Stalin's secret police. This could have only one result: alienation set in very quickly, leaving German units to operate as 'strangers in a strange land', unable to relax even in rear areas, where heavy partisan activity soon arose. In retrospect, with a little more care and compassion, the Germans might have avoided this to their own considerable benefit.

Above: Motorcycle troops, distinctive in their rubberized coats, react to enemy fire from the buildings in the background, Russia, 1942. The soldier standing on the left is returning fire, while his comrades are more cautious; he is wearing the motorcyclists' coat buttoned around his legs to form coveralls.

But it was not only the people who appeared strange. Just as shocking to German soldiers was the nature of the terrain, especially as they travelled deeper into the Soviet Union. During the early months of the Barbarossa campaign, for example, the forests, rivers and rolling grasslands may have been seen as no

more than picturesque, but as time went on, the sheer enormity and emptiness of Russia, particularly in the south, began to eat away at morale. Many German first-hand accounts make the point that serving in the Ukraine was depressing, not because of the fighting (although that was often bitter) but because one could travel literally for days without the scenery changing – just mile after endless mile of wide open steppes, dotted with small villages and isolated farms. To soldiers used to the much closer and ordered country of the west, it was as if they were travelling to the ends of the world, with civilization fading away behind them. The lack of roads and the ubiquitous dust of summer merely made the image more surreal. To their compatriots further north, the brooding menace of the Pripet Marshes or the dark forests of the Baltic states had much the same impact.

All of these problems were exacerbated once the weather broke in October 1941. The rains came suddenly, catching many German units unprepared for the transformation of dust into deep mud, but this was nothing compared to the onset of the frosts and

Above: *The business-end of a 7.92mm schwere Maschinengewehr 34 heavy machine gun, well emplaced in a sheltered position in Russia, 1942. Mounted on a special Lafette 34 tripod, the weapon is configured for sustained long-range firing in support of infantry attacks.*

Above: *The crew of a pristine mittlerer Schutzenpanzerwagen (Sd Kfz) 251/7 engineer vehicle watch as Waffen-SS colleagues clear a fallen tree, probably felled by partisans as a roadblock. The Sd Kfz 251/7 carried a crew of eight.*

Right: *Observation of the enemy was vital, both to warn of impending attacks and to check for new defensive positions. Here, a group of infantry soldiers uses the roof of a peasant hut in the Ukraine as an ideal location.*

Left: The danger of partisan attack was ever-present in the rear areas on the Eastern Front, especially close to the railways that formed the vital logistic link between Germany and the frontline. Any Russians found in the vicinity, such as this girl, needed to be carefully checked out.

Right: Caught in the middle of the fighting on the Eastern Front were the ordinary peasants, scared and confused by the savage nature of the battles around them. As a German patrol moves forward in the Ukraine, they stop to interrogate one of the locals. He seems prepared to help.

Right: By 1943, the Germans are in trouble on the Eastern Front, being forced back by overwhelming Soviet forces. Here, two infantrymen pull back from a village close to Kharkov, leaving the buildings ablaze behind them. They are carrying what they can salvage – in this case, grenades and ammunition.

snow a few weeks later. Vehicles bogged down in mud became locked in the frozen ground – some had to be freed using dynamite – and the soldiers suffered all the effects of unprecedented cold. If the fighting had ceased at that point and the Germans had been able to go into 'winter quarters', the situation might have been manageable, but the Soviets seemed less affected and made sure that their ability to survive (and fight) was exploited to the full. As it was, many German units found it impossible to operate in the depths of winter: soldiers literally froze to death on guard duty or lost the use of limbs through frostbite, vehicles refused to start and vital equipment ceased to function. When it is added that winter clothing was not on general issue in 1941, partly because

of the mistaken belief that the campaign would be over before the need for it arose and partly because of a failure of the supply chain from Germany, it can readily be appreciated that life for the ordinary soldier was extreme. If he survived, he deserved his 'Order of the Frozen Meat'.

On top of all this, of course, was the actual fighting. From the start, this was of a style and bitterness not experienced in previous campaigns. Tough battles may have been fought on occasions in Poland or the west, but generally speaking they had been conducted in a 'civilized' manner, with the surrender of enemy soldiers accepted and the wounded cared for. There were exceptions – Waffen-SS units had gained a reputation for ruthlessness, not

least when they shot British prisoners in the advance towards Dunkirk in late May 1940 – but the rules of war were usually obeyed. The same was not true in the east. Hitler's infamous 'Commissar Order' of June 1941, directing the immediate execution of all captured political commissars, was indicative of the totality of the campaign and, despite a widespread belief that such orders were largely ignored by all but the SS, recent historical research suggests strongly that most Wehrmacht units carried them out. In response, the Soviets quickly became just as ruthless, torturing or executing prisoners on a regular basis.

The war of atrocities

On both sides there was a general disregard for the rights of PoWs. Few of the estimated two million Soviet soldiers captured in 1941 survived the war – many died of disease or starvation in prison camps, others were worked to death as slave labour in Germany's war-factories – and the same fate awaited those German soldiers who were unfortunate enough to fall into Soviet hands. By the same token, neither side showed a great deal of compassion towards enemy wounded; if they could not march into captivity, they were often shot where they lay.

Above: At certain times in the year - spring and autumn - the rains came down, turning tracks and roads to mud along the length of the Eastern Front. When this happened, motorized traffic came to a standstill unless helped by more traditional means. Horses hitched to a motorcycle was one solution.

This was reflected in the nature of the fighting, for if soldiers knew or suspected that they would be ill-treated, they fought more tenaciously just to survive. During the early months of Barbarossa, such an attitude affected the Germans less than their enemies, for obvious reasons, but this changed as the winter set in. Isolated by the weather and the emptiness of the terrain, German units would suddenly find themselves under attack from hordes of ill-equipped but adequately clothed enemy troops, and would be forced to fight hand-to-hand battles in the snow, often using sharpened entrenching tools and bayonets as the only weapons unaffected by the cold.

If the Germans won, the survivors would immediately strip Soviet bodies of their clothing – white oversuits and felt boots were the favourite pieces of booty – and exchange their own weapons for enemy weapons. The Soviet PPSh-41 submachine

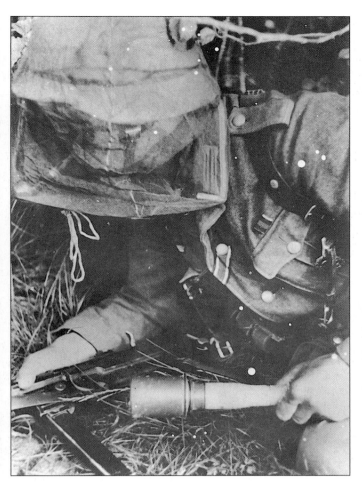

gun, for example, was preferred to the German MP40 for the simple reason that it was less prone to jamming because of the cold, being of more simple design and manufacture. By December 1941, special orders had to be issued by Wehrmacht command to ensure that soldiers returning to Germany on leave were issued with new uniforms before they left Russia; German civilians had apparently been shocked by the ragged and unconventional appearance of some of the men.

Left: One of the problems encountered by German troops in southern Russia was marshy terrain, often containing swarms of malaria-spreading mosquitoes. This soldier, equipped with an MP 40 submachine gun and Stielhandgranate 39 hand grenade, is wearing a specially designed helmet net.

Below: As artillery fire comes down in the woods in front of them, a machine-gun crew waits for enemy infantry to attack, northern Russia, 1943. The gun is a 7.92mm Maschinengewehr 42, the highly effective successor to the MG 34, which incorporated a recoil-operated roller locking system.

Pages 98-99: An arresting image of war on the Eastern Front – a German infantry section, with the three-man crew of an MG 34 in the centre, follows its officer and his radio-man (on the right) along a dusty road in high summer. The photograph was probably taken in July or August 1942.

As the winter of 1941-42 dragged on, the Wehrmacht did begin to adapt. Soldiers learned to build special shelters in the snow, piling it up to act as a windbreak, or merely evicted Russian peasants from their hovels and took them over, transforming them into havens of warmth and security. Equally, the lack of warm clothing led to improvisations, ranging from packing boots with newspaper to the wearing of as many layers of clothing as possible.

Soldiers also learned what not to do. If they touched bare metal with unprotected hands, the flesh would freeze and be ripped off. Men could not be expected to stand guard for longer than 30 minutes without feeling the full effects of the cold. Movement away from shelters was tantamount to suicide. They even took some

Above: Despite images of the German Army as a highly mechanized and fast-moving organization, the reality was always different. The vast bulk of the army moved by more traditional means - on its feet, on horseback or, as shown here, on bicycles. Good progress could be made on firm roads.

comfort from the fact that all around them men were suffering equally. The heavy casualties suffered during Barbarossa may have left yawning gaps in the ranks of certain units, not least the panzer divisions, but those who survived were undoubtedly sustained by the bonds of comradeship that continued to exist and were enhanced by common experience.

Above: An infantry lieutenant leads his men out of a Russian village to conduct a patrol, reading orders as he goes. The NCO behind him consults a map. The ground is muddy, implying that the photograph was taken in the spring, although the soldiers are on solid ground.

Right: An NCO and his driver struggle to free their BMW R-75 motorcycle combination from the glutinous mud of a Russian autumn, 1942. Movement in such conditions was impossible although, if vehicles were not stuck fast, they could move once the mud froze solid.

Certain lessons emerged from the campaign. As the fighting grew more bitter, so did the attitude of the German soldier to his enemy, leading to a belief that this was a war to the death. Men became hardened to the conditions and to the realities of battle in ways that would have been impossible in earlier operations. They also learned to look after themselves and not to depend on a supply chain that was constantly struggling to operate, let alone deliver the right equipment to the right place at the right time. Many soldiers followed the pattern of the peasants around them, living as they did and eating the same food, inadequate though that might have seemed when they first entered Russia. They also insisted on better clothing and equipment now that the campaign was clearly going to be long. If snowsuits and felt boots were desirable, it was obviously better if they were on issue from the Wehrmacht rather than dependent on captured stocks; similarly, if Soviet weapons were superior, German equivalents should be developed and provided. Nor was this confined to small arms like the PPSh-41.

New German tank designs

One of the real shocks the Germans experienced in 1941 had been the radical nature of the T-34 tank, with its sloped armour and 76mm gun, for the Germans had nothing equivalent in their inventory. Less than half of the panzers used at the start of Barbarossa were of the best German types, the Mark IIIs and IVs, and although they had proved remarkably robust – some of them travelled well over 1000 miles (1600km) without a major overhaul – they were outclassed by the T-34.

One of the results was that German designers began to copy key features of the Soviet machine, experimenting with tanks that

Above: Gebirgsjager (mountain troop) officers inspect captured Soviet small arms after an engagement in the Caucasus, 1942. The lieutenant in the centre is looking at a 7.62mm Tokarev SVT-40 automatic rifle, while other examples of the same weapon lie on the ground.

Right: A Goliath remotely controlled demolition device is prepared for action, 1943. The Goliath was often used to attack enemy tanks as well as to clear obstacles: if the device could be positioned beneath the tank and then detonated, it could have a dramatically destructive effect.

would appear from winter 1942 and summer 1943 respectively as the Mark V Panther and Mark VI Tiger. Both were excellent fighting vehicles – the Panther with its sloped armour and 75mm gun, the Tiger with its all-powerful 88mm main armament – but they represented a significant shift in German capability on the battlefield. Earlier panzers had the advantage of being fast, enabling them to exploit gaps in enemy defences; the new designs were bigger, heavier and, of course, less manoeuvrable, cutting down the opportunities for blitzkrieg-style advances. At the same time, recognition that towed artillery had always lagged behind the tanks led the Germans to develop self-propelled guns (usually no more than a field gun mounted on a panzer chassis) which, despite their impact, were still incapable of achieving speed. In short, the 1941-42 campaign in Russia initiated a process of transforming the Wehrmacht from a fast-moving, offensive force to one that was powerful in defence but slow.

This transformation may not have been immediately apparent once the winter passed and Hitler turned his thoughts to a new spring offensive in 1942, but it was happening nonetheless. As the survivors of the winter nightmare emerged from their shelters to face the welcoming return of warmer weather, they represented a new army, hardened to the realities of war in Russia and to the prospect of continued fighting with weapons that may have been improved but were also less flexible. The results would soon be apparent for all to see.

Above: A German horse-mounted messenger races past the burning remains of a Soviet Bystrochodniya Tankov (BT, or 'Fast Tank'), armed with a 45mm main gun. Although it is difficult to tell because of the smoke, this may be a BA-6 armoured-car version of the BT, mounted on wheels rather than tracks.

Below: Standing guard over the railways was an onerous but very necessary duty on the Eastern Front, for they were the only bulk-carrying logistic link available. Partisan attacks increased in intensity after 1941; this photograph indicates just how vulnerable the railways were to such interdiction.

CHAPTER 7
STALINGRAD

The German 1942 campaign to seize the oilfields of the Caucasus and the industrial and armaments centre of Stalingrad would lead to the destruction of the German Sixth Army in one of the most savage battles of the war.

Left: Infantry soldiers rush forward with ammunition supplies during the German Summer Offensive of 1942.

Above: To begin with the Germans achieved some success, reaching the Don and taking thousands of prisoners.

Hitler's strategic plan for 1942 was ambitious. Recognizing that the conflict would now be long, and that he faced the potential nightmare of a war on two fronts simultaneously – the Soviets in the east and the Anglo-Americans in the west – the Führer was aware that Germany needed access to certain raw materials if the country was to survive. High on the list was oil, for although German scientists had begun to produce synthetic fuels from coal, the process was laborious and the results less than satisfactory. Some oilfields were within the Axis empire, in Rumania and Hungary, but the real prize lay in the Caucasus, tantalizingly

close to the highwater mark of the advance into southern Russia in 1941. Nor would a seizure of the Caucasus just produce oil; if German troops could move south towards the Turkish border, hitherto neutral Turkey might be persuaded to join the Axis alliance, opening up the possibility of a further advance deep into the Middle East.

It all looked simple on paper. An advance towards the River Don, to the north of the major industrial, communications and armaments centre of Stalingrad, would protect the left flank of the main assault in the direction of the oilfields and Turkish frontier.

Above: German infantry wade across a small river in the Kuban, to the south of Rostov, summer 1942. All are wearing what was termed 'assault equipment', including messtins, rolled waterproofs, gas masks and water bottles, attached to their webbing straps. Note the 50-round drum magazine on the MG 34 machine gun.

Right: Three infantrymen discuss the next move in their offensive into the Caucasus, summer 1942. In the background, smoke billows from oil refineries set on fire by the retreating Soviets, suggesting that the photograph was taken close to the high water mark of the German advance. The main oilfields were never captured.

Bottom right: Stalingrad burns as the Germans approach the city in September 1942. The Sixth Army, accompanied by elements of the Fourth Panzer Army, initially had no intention of getting sucked into urban fighting; they preferred to call in artillery and air strikes in the hope that the Soviets would retreat.

Bottom left: Pz Kpfw IIIs of the 24th Panzer Division cross the River Don near Voronezh by means of a pontoon bridge, early July 1942. The bleakness of the terrain is apparent, affording little protection. Note the divisional sign on the right-rear of the nearest tank.

Left: *Street fighting begins in Stalingrad, September 1942. The armoured vehicle is a Soviet self-propelled gun on the chassis of a Komsomolets artillery tractor, an effective combination in close-quarter combat, but here rather wasted by being caught in the open. The building in the background shows signs of savage battle.*

Top right: *A machine gunner fires his MG 34 from an improvised position on a street corner in the outskirts of Stalingrad, September 1942. The buildings around him are less substantial than those in the centre of the city and are not destined to survive for very long. The battle is only just beginning.*

Bottom right: *Stalingrad was a modern city, largely rebuilt on Stalin's orders in the 1930s as a 'showpiece' of Soviet communism. This is indicated by the nature of the buildings about to be assaulted in this photograph – they are substantial, brick-built edifices, ideal for defence and difficult to destroy.*

The Soviets, still shielding Moscow, would be caught unawares and a major German victory would be ensured. But such a plan required careful preparation, something that Adolf Hitler, now acting as commander-in-chief, proved incapable of organizing. He was obsessed with minor tactical problems that made his planning conferences increasingly irrelevant, yet convinced that he and only he had the strategic grasp that would ensure final victory, and as a result the direction of the war on the Eastern Front drifted into chaos. Commanders on the ground were subjected to constant interference from the Führer's headquarters, and orders were changed apparently on the whim of one man, operating hundreds of miles to the rear.

Operation Blue begins

This was not obvious to begin with. The new offensive, codenamed Operation Blue, opened on 28 June 1942, when Army Group South pushed forward from a line between Kursk and Kharkov to assault the city of Voronezh on the Don. After heavy fighting, caused in part by Stalin's belief that this was a preliminary to an attack on Moscow from the south, Voronezh fell on 5 July, by which time a subsidiary (but no less bitterly fought) campaign had finally cleared the Crimea, taking Sevastopol and pushing Soviet forces out of the Kerch Peninsula. However, these were only the opening moves. On 9 July, Hitler split Army Group South into two new formations, Army Group A and Army Group B, and gave each new objectives. As Army Group B, which included those forces already engaged around Voronezh, thrust down the Donets Corridor towards Stalingrad, Army Group A was to capture the Donets Basin to the north of Rostov before advancing south into the Caucasus with the intention of consolidating a line from Batumi to Baku.

Above: Substantial areas of Stalingrad were soon reduced to rubble by artillery and air attacks. Far from making the German task easier, these attacks left piles of broken bricks that blocked the streets, making movement virtually impossible, and allowed the surviving Soviets to establish strong defensive positions in the ruins.

Right: A German infantry squad marches past burnt-out vehicles and blazing buildings in a residential quarter of Stalingrad, October 1942. They are moving to join other infantrymen in the street beyond, prior to an assault on Soviet positions deeper in the city. It is very dissimilar to a blitzkrieg advance.

Army Group B made rapid progress, leading Hitler to make the first of a number of far-reaching decisions. On 16 July, he ordered Fourth Panzer Army to leave Army Group B and move south to help First Panzer Army in the assault on the Caucasus. This was a mistake, reducing Army Group B's advance to the pace of the infantry belonging to General Friedrich Paulus's Sixth Army, now approaching the city of Stalingrad. Situated on a bend in the River Volga, the city jutted out to create a potential base for Soviet counter-attacks towards Rostov, which might cut off Army Group A in the Caucasus. On 30 July, Hitler countermanded his previous orders and moved Fourth Panzer Army back north, intent on using it to spearhead an advance on Stalingrad itself. This decision meant that the Germans were now pursuing two objectives – Stalingrad and the oilfields – and were incapable of taking either.

Fourth Panzer Army was effectively removed from the offensive for about two weeks, as it marched and counter-marched in response to changing orders, and this left both Army Groups significantly weakened. Moreover, despite some rapid gains when Fourth Panzer finally rejoined Sixth Army, the Soviets had recognized the nature of the threat and made moves to shore up their defences. German momentum was lost.

The Sixth Army reaches Stalingrad

Paulus entered the suburbs of Stalingrad on 23/24 August 1942, only to find that resistance had stiffened. Meanwhile, further south, Army Group A had taken Stavropol on 5 August and Krasnodar four days later, but could make little additional progress. With its troops close to exhaustion and its supply lines hopelessly stretched, Army Group A stalled. It was a classic example of an overall commander (in this case Hitler) ignoring the mili-

Above: A 2 cm Flugabwehrkanone (Flak) 30 in action in the ruins of Stalingrad, 1942. Such weapons could be used in the ground-support role, lending fire to infantry assaults. The angle at which the soldiers on the left are using a rangefinder and binoculars suggests that the target is in the buildings beyond.

tary maxim that the aim of an offensive must be maintained, otherwise confusion will reign and objectives will prove impossible to attain. The Germans under Paulus were about to discover the consequences of Hitler's error.

The Red Army's counter-attack

Stalingrad, a model city named after the ruler of the Soviet Union, stretched north-south along the west bank of the Volga, providing a strong frontage to the enemy but little real depth. If the Soviets lost the west bank, they had nowhere else to go and would be forced to pull back, leaving the Germans with the freedom to reassemble their forces for a more concerted thrust towards the oilfields. Stalin recognized this and, the honour of his name apart, insisted that the city be defended to the death. In this, the Soviet Sixty-Second and Sixty-Fourth Armies enjoyed certain advantages – they knew the ground intimately and could make the most of factories and other buildings to create solid blocks in the path of their enemy – but they were also hampered by poor command and by the need to bring all supplies and reinforcements across the Volga under German fire. It was going to be a tough contest, the outcome of which would decide the future shape of the entire campaign in the east.

Paulus made his first move into Stalingrad on 7 September, aiming to split the city in two and reach the banks of the Volga.

He made some progress, aided by the Luftwaffe, which flew mission after mission to destroy the urban centre, and by the tanks of Fourth Panzer Army, which advanced into the old part of the city in the south, splitting the Soviet defences. On 10 September, however, Stalin appointed General Vasili Chuikov to command the Sixty-Second Army. Although the situation looked hopeless, Chuikov boosted the morale of the defenders by appearing personally in their midst and vowing publicly that he would remain until the Germans had been evicted. Few can have believed him at that stage, but signs of Soviet strength were beginning to emerge. The ability of small groups of Soviet soldiers to defend selected locations – notably the Red October, Barrikady and Tractor factories in the northern part of the city and a huge concrete grain elevator further south – against seemingly overwhelming odds was already apparent.

The Soviets were aided by the fact that urban fighting denied to the Germans the thing that they were best at: the creation and maintenance of momentum. Instead of causing collapse through the sudden appearance of panzers deep in the enemy rear, the

Right: The crew of a German light anti-tank gun stare out over a winter landscape, December 1942. Although better equipped to withstand the cold in this, the second winter on the Eastern Front, the soldiers are operating at the end of a stretched supply line, far from home.

Below: Horse-drawn sledges provided one of the few means of movement for the vast bulk of the German Army on the Eastern Front during the winter months. By now – 1942 – the horses are looking distinctly bedraggled, although the soldiers attending them have received proper winter clothing.

Wehrmacht was having to shift the emphasis of its combat effort to the infantry. With engineer support, it was they who entered the factories and it was they who fought floor by floor and room by room through the ruins of the bombed and battered city. Their daily progress was often measured in yards, each one of which was exacting a terrible toll.

By mid-September, Sixth Army had occupied most of the old city in the south, but was becoming dangerously exposed in a salient, centred on Stalingrad, the flanks of which were weakly defended by Rumanian, Hungarian and Italian troops, spread thinly and suffering from poor morale. The Soviets monitored this.

While fixing Paulus inside Stalingrad, they prepared to strike the flanks of the German advance, aiming to encircle Sixth Army (plus the greater part of Fourth Panzer) and cut it off from its supply links to the west. By late October, the broad nature of the counter-offensive, code-named Operation Uranus, had been finalized: to the north of Stalingrad, reserves belonging to the South-West and Don Fronts (a Front was the equivalent of a west-

ern Army Group) would push south-eastwards through the Rumanian Third Army to link up at Kalach with units of the Stalingrad Front attacking through the Rumanian Fourth Army from the south. These forces would then create a barrier against any German attempts at counter-attack from outside, while squeezing the Stalingrad pocket. At the same time, Chuikov would intensify his efforts, tying Paulus down to prevent him from counter-attacking from within.

The Soviet assault began on 19 November 1942. Within four days, the Rumanians in the north had cracked apart, allowing the Soviet Fifth Tank Army to reach Kalach against crumbling opposition. On 23 November, elements of the Fifty-First Army linked up,

Below: *A Pz Kpfw III moves into a Russian village during the winter fighting around Stalingrad, December 1942. Once the ground had frozen, tanks could move with a degree of freedom, but were dependent on a supply chain that was heavily disrupted by winter conditions.*

Above: Once Stalingrad had been surrounded in November 1942, the German troops trapped inside faced deteriorating conditions, coinciding with the onset of winter. Short of supplies and, as time went on without relief, bereft of hope, they struggled to survive. It was a nightmare existence.

Below: Being wounded in battle is always traumatic, but to go through the experience in the depths of a Russian winter, with little hope of evacuation, made it something to be contemplated with horror. This soldier is being dragged away on an improvised sledge by his comrades; his prospects of survival are slim.

creating an enormous pocket within which nearly 250,000 German troops were trapped. Paulus was refused permission by Hitler to attempt a breakout – something that stood a good chance of success at this early stage – and was ordered instead to maintain his positions inside Stalingrad. Supplies, it was announced, would be flown in by the Luftwaffe and a counter-attack mounted from outside to smash the new Soviet positions. Neither policy worked.

Paulus's men needed a minimum of 600 tons of supplies a day just to survive, yet the Luftwaffe, feeling the impact of the Ju-52 losses over Crete and during the winter of 1941-42 on the Eastern Front, could manage less than 100 tons, condemning Sixth Army to starvation. At the same time, General Erich von Manstein, newly promoted to command the hastily created Army Group Don, failed to achieve the promised relief. His offensive, code-named Operation Winter Storm, opened on 12 December with an advance by about 230 tanks of LVII Panzer Corps; although they managed to get to within 30 miles (50km) of the Stalingrad perimeter, Paulus refused to break out to link up with them. Under mounting pressure from Hitler, who was beginning to view the battle for Stalingrad as something of a symbolic and personal crusade, Paulus remained fixed firmly in the ruins of the city. There, his soldiers occupied whatever positions they could and tried to survive as the winter weather arrived. They were doomed to destruction.

Further attacks by the Soviets routed the Italian Eighth Army on the Don in mid-December, leaving von Manstein's flank exposed.

He had no choice but to pull back, despite a realization (not shared by Hitler) that Sixth Army could not survive against the combination of Soviet pressure and winter conditions. Christmas messages, including a personal one from the Führer, were broadcast to Paulus's men by radio, but most of them knew that they were trapped. Huddled in cellars for warmth and in an effort to escape the Soviet artillery, they penned their last letters home and waited for the inevitable. It was not long in coming.

Soviet reserves, crossing the Volga to reinforce Chuikov's decimated units, pressed in from the east, while units from Operation Uranus squeezed in from the west. The airfield, the last remaining contact with home, soon fell amid scenes of chaos, as wounded and fit together tried desperately to board the last transport aircraft; demoralized, frozen and injured men either succumbed to the cold or surrendered to the advancing Soviets.

On 26 January 1943, units of the Don Front linked up with Chuikov's Sixty-Second Army in the centre of Stalingrad, splinter-ing what remained of the German defences. On 31 January Hitler, in a last-ditch effort to ensure continued resistance, promoted Paulus to the rank of field marshal, knowing that Paulus would remember that no German soldier of such exalted rank had ever been taken alive in battle, but it was all to no avail. Later on the same day, Paulus – thin, unshaven and thoroughly demoralized – sought terms for his surviving men. The last of them surrendered on 2 February 1943.

Stalingrad – the turning point

Over 200,000 German soldiers were killed or captured during the Stalingrad battles. Of the 91,000 who marched – or, more accurately, shuffled – into Soviet captivity, less than 5000 of them were to survive the experience and return to Germany 10 years later, falling to disease, exhaustion and harsh treatment by their captors. They represented the cream of the Wehrmacht infantry, the loss of whom was to be sorely felt in the months to come. Stalingrad may not have seen the end of German offensive capability – that was to come at Kursk in July 1943 – but it was a turning point nonetheless. The Soviets gave notice at Stalingrad that they had not only recovered from the shock of Barbarossa, but that they were also fully capable of playing the Germans at their own game. The only problem for Hitler was that they were already better at it than he was.

Below: A Pz Kpfw III, fitted with a short-barrelled 50mm main armament, crunches forward over firm snow, Eastern Front, early 1943. Despite being well out-gunned by the Soviet T-34 at this stage of the war, the Pz Kpfw III was still useful for infantry support. Note that the crew has not painted out the recognition cross on the side of the hull.

CHAPTER 8

KURSK

Operation Citadel, the German offensive at Kursk in July 1943, was the greatest tank battle in history. By the end of the two-week battle, the Wehrmacht's strategic offensive capability on the Eastern Front was lost.

Left: The crew of a Pz Kpfw IV rest before battle, Russia, 1943. The bareheaded crew member is seated on the 75mm gun.

Above: A Pz Kpfw V Ausf A Panther (left), parked next to an Sd Kfz 251 half-track, Kursk sector, June 1943.

Once the Soviets had encircled Stalingrad in November 1942, Army Group A in the Caucasus was vulnerable. If the Stalingrad Front could advance to liberate Rostov, at the northeastern tip of the Sea of Azov, the link between Army Group A and its supplies further north would be cut, forcing a retreat or collapse. This was obvious to anyone who consulted a map, yet Hitler was extremely reluctant to order a withdrawal away from the impending danger. Only after Army Group A had been attacked by the Soviet Trans-Caucasus Front on 19 November, precipitating more than a month of hard fighting, did he change his mind. In late December, as Sixth Army faced annihilation in the Stalingrad pocket, over 250,000 German troops finally pulled back north in the Caucasus, entering the Taman Peninsula and

forging tenuous links with their compatriots in the Crimea. At the same time, other German troops fought a series of bitter engagements to protect Rostov. The city fell on 14 February 1943, but they gained sufficient time to ensure the comparative safety of Army Group A.

This was just as well, for elsewhere on the Eastern Front the Germans were facing renewed Soviet onslaughts. Even before Stalingrad had fallen, General Filip Golikov's Voronezh Front attacked westwards, liberating the city of Kursk on 8 February and thrusting towards the industrial centre at Kharkov. The Soviet advance was rapid but poorly coordinated, creating a salient around Kursk that protruded deep into German lines. Hitler, noting this, ordered Kharkov to be held as the southern shoulder of

Left: Despite the setbacks at Stalingrad and Kharkov in early 1943, there was still a degree of optimism in the Wehrmacht as soldiers prepared for the offensive at Kursk. This machine gunner, carrying an MG 34, is sufficiently confident to smile cheerily for the camera. However, the mood would not last much longer.

Right: A rare action shot, taken during the Battle of Kursk, July 1943. As infantry soldiers dig in on a ridge line to provide cover, elements of a panzer regiment, equipped with Pz Kpfw IIIs, deploy along the road axis in the valley. The vulnerability of tanks to air attack can be appreciated.

Right: German infantry, accompanied by tanks of Fourth Panzer Army, advance towards Prokhorovka, Kursk offensive, July 1943. All are wearing helmet camouflage covers and the man in the lead is carrying a Tellermine (Tmi) 42 anti-tank mine. The tanks are Pz Kpfw IIIs, that on the right with a long-barrelled 50mm gun.

the salient, prior to a counter-attack to pinch the whole salient out. He ordered forward the elite of his troops – Lieutenant General Paul Hausser's II SS Corps – and committed them to the defence of Kharkov. They entered a maelstrom of fighting amid the ruins which even the SS could not withstand. Despite direct orders from Hitler to hold firm, Hausser realized that his corps was about to be destroyed. On 15 February he withdrew through the only remaining corridor, leaving the Soviets to re-take the city.

The Germans retake Kharkov

Hitler, predictably, was furious, but Field Marshal von Manstein, commanding the recently reconstituted Army Group South, defused his anger by suggesting that the time was ripe for a counter-attack designed to catch over-extended Soviet spearheads and crush them using fast-moving panzer formations. Known in retrospect as 'mobile defence', the tactic worked. Hausser halted his withdrawal at Krasnograd on 19 February and, in company with what remained of Fourth Panzer Army, suddenly turned on the pursuing enemy. The Soviet spearheads were caught by surprise. Over 23,000

Right: *A 150mm schwere Feldhaubitze 18 heavy artillery piece in action, Kursk sector, summer 1943. The stockpile of shells in the foreground implies the beginning of a sustained bombardment, in which case the crew will have their work cut out. All except the firer are protecting their ears from the noise.*

Red Army troops were killed and nearly 9000 captured, forcing Golikov to pull back in disarray. He abandoned Kharkov to the Germans for the third time in 18 months, but von Manstein was careful not to make the same error as his enemy. Aware that the spring thaw was about to turn relatively firm, frozen ground to mud, stopping all advances, he consolidated his gains and set up a defensive line. Some Soviet units thrust northwestwards in the direction of Belgorod, but by late March 1943, as winter came to an end, all mobility ceased.

The Kursk salient remained as a tempting target for a sustained German counter-attack. Its shoulders – Orel in the north and Kharkov in the south – were in German hands, while an estimated 1.3 million Soviet troops, including some of the best formations belonging to the Red Army, were packed within its boundaries.

Left: Infantry pause to refresh themselves, having marched through the heat of a Russian summer towards the frontline at Kursk, July 1943. The Obergefreiter (Corporal) on the right is carrying an MG 34 machine gun. In the background is a Pz Kpfw VI Ausf F Tiger I, fitted with a formidable 88mm KwK 36 main gun.

Right: A Soviet tank commander is hauled out of the turret of his knocked-out T-34/76 by the crew of an assault gun (indicated by their field-grey panzer uniforms) who, presumably, are responsible for the 'kill', Kursk, July 1943. The bandaged German crewman is holding a 9mm Walther Pistole 38 in case of trouble.

Bottom left: Russian peasants – suspected partisans or conscripted labourers – watch with interest as elements of a German reconnaissance unit deploy. The armoured cars are an Sd Kfz 231 (left), two Sd Kfz 232 (Fu) radio vehicles (with the distinctive roof aerials) and an Sd Kfz 221 (parked beyond the 231 on the right). It is a fascinating combination.

Left: *A knocked-out Soviet T-34/76 tank, photographed at Kursk, July 1943. Minus its left-hand track and riddled with bullet holes, it makes a forlorn sight, but its loss would hardly have been felt. Soviet tank production by 1943 was reaching its peak and the crews were always expendable.*

Below right: *Aftermath of the tank battle at Prokhorovka, July 1943: in the foreground, and extending almost to the horizon, are the remains of Soviet T-34s, destroyed as they encountered the armour of the SS Panzer Divisions. It was the biggest tank battle in history and, despite these losses, one that resulted in Soviet victory.*

The salient was by no means small – 160 miles (225km) from north to south – but it seemed ripe for a pincer attack designed to squeeze it out and so destroy the cream of Stalin's spearheads. Some historians have argued that if Hitler had concentrated on such an attack in February or March 1943, catching the enemy before he had consolidated, then he might have enjoyed success. As it was, he waited until early July, giving Stalin ample time in which to prepare.

Hitler had his reasons for delay. During February and March, more important battles were being fought around Kharkov and as soon as they were over, the spring thaw precluded mobile warfare. More crucially, the Führer was insistent that the counter-

attack should be decisive, and that new, more powerful weapons should be fielded (at the end of January 1943 there were only 495 battleworthy German tanks on the Eastern Front). These included the Panzer Mark V Panther and Mark VI Tiger, as well as the first of a new generation of self-propelled and assault guns, including the Ferdinand (later called the Elefant), based on the Tiger tank chassis, specifically designed to break through heavily defended positions. In itself, the decision was sound, but production delays, caused by a combination of development problems (especially with the Panther) and Allied bombing of factories in Germany, meant that it took time for the required forces to be concentrated. An assault much before early July was virtually impossible.

Stalin made the most of the delay. Details of the forthcoming offensive, code-named Operation Zitadelle (Citadel), were fed to him via the 'Lucy' spy ring in Switzerland, apparently from a disaffected source in OKH, although some now believe that this was a 'front' used by the western Allies to pass intelligence to Moscow that had been gained from Enigma decrypts, without alerting Stalin to its origins. Whatever the truth of the matter, the information was invaluable, enabling Soviet commanders to make elaborate preparations. The Kursk salient was transformed into a huge defended 'box', with the emphasis on the shoulders where the German attacks would come. Civilians from Kursk and its surrounding area were mobilized to dig anti-tank obstacles and gun emplacements; infantry armed with anti-tank guns and mines were deployed forward to blunt the forthcoming assault; more than 5000 tanks were kept back as a counter-stroke force to hit any German spearheads that penetrated the front line. In some places, the defences were nearly 120 miles (190km) in depth, presenting attackers with a 'chequer-board' of obstacles that were guaranteed to prevent the creation of momentum. Zitadelle may have been an elaborately planned offensive, but it was doomed from the start; blitzkrieg was about to meet its match.

Above: The crew of a 50mm Panzerabwehrkanone (Pak) 38 anti-tank gun in action at the Battle of Kursk, July 1943. Introduced in 1941 as a replacement to the 37mm Pak 35/36, the Pak 38 was a well designed and effective weapon. Its tungsten-core AP40 shells could penetrate almost all types of Allied and Soviet armour.

None of this was known during the weeks leading up to the opening of the offensive, although some German commanders suspected a trap. Even if they did not, they were aware that the formations being concentrated to the north and south of the salient were the best available, the loss of which would be catastrophic. In the north, the German Ninth Army, part of Field Marshal Gunther von Kluge's Army Group Centre, deployed 21 divisions, of which 6 were panzer and 1 panzergrenadier, with a total of nearly 800 tanks available. In the south, the reconstituted Fourth Panzer Army, part of von Manstein's Army Group South, had 22 divisions, 6 of which were panzer and 5 panzergrenadier,

Above: *A German Pz Kpfw IV Ausf F2. Despite the Tigers and Panthers which fought at Kursk, the mainstay of the German panzer arm was still the Panzer IV. The difference between the F1 and F2 versions related largely to the introduction of the new 75mm KwK40 main gun.*

Right: *The distinctive turret of a Soviet T-34/85 is all that identifies this victim of dive-bomber attack. The appearance of the T-34/85, which combined the manoeuvrability of the T-34 with the 85mm cannon, took the Germans by surprise.*

with a total of nearly 1300 tanks in the front line. Together, the two armies held an estimated 70 per cent of the German armoured strength then on the Eastern Front, representing a formidable but potentially vulnerable concentration of force. If these units were lost, there was little left in reserve.

Above: Three of the four crew-members of a 75mm Pak 40/2 Sd Kfz 131 Marder II heavy anti-tank self-propelled gun pose for the camera, Eastern Front, 1943. The 19 'kill' rings painted on the barrel, and the medals displayed by the rather ostentatious commander, imply that this vehicle has seen extensive action.

Operation Citadel commences

The 'Lucy' spy ring warned the Soviets that Zitadelle would begin early on 5 July 1943; the Soviet response was to lay down a sudden artillery bombardment just before the attack was due, disrupting German moves and giving notice that surprise – one of the key ingredients of successful blitzkrieg – had not been achieved. The psychological impact was significant, but it did not prevent the attacks taking place. In the north, Ninth Army fought hard to penetrate the enemy defences, only to get bogged down less than four miles from their start lines. In the south, Fourth Panzer Army fared a little better, advancing up to eight miles (13km) on the first day in places, but it was obvious that momentum could not be gained. As dozens of panzers and self-propelled guns, accompanied by panzergrenadiers and engineers, inched forward, they found their progress blocked by dug-in T-34s or anti-tank guns. As soon as they dealt with the immediate threat, they encountered more of the same, forcing them to probe backwards, forwards and sideways in a vain effort to find a 'line of least resistance' that just did not exist.

Nor could the Luftwaffe help in the ways it had in the past. Although the Red Air Force did not enjoy complete air superiority

over the battle area – it was still possible, for example, for the Germans to use Stuka dive-bombers on the first day – they were still up in sufficient strength to inflict damage of their own. Their Ilyushin Il-2 Sturmovik attack aircraft, specially designed for close support of ground forces, flew in packs, protected by fighters, seeking out German armour and destroying it in 'circle of death' formations which involved the continuous commitment of squadrons hour after hour. One German panzer division lost nearly 20 of its fighting vehicles in a single day to these means.

The battle quickly degenerated into an attritional slogging match, with the Germans incapable of making significant progress. After almost a week, the two pincers were still the best part of 140 miles (225km) apart, although on 11 July it did seem as if a breakthrough was imminent in the south. Tanks of the 1st, 2nd and 3rd SS Panzer Divisions, committed en masse, suddenly found the defences thinning out around the village of Prokhorovka, on the main rail line linking Belgorod and Kursk. It was a Soviet trap.

As the Tigers nosed forward along the side of the railway, gradually assuming a modicum of speed, they were suddenly confronted, early on 12 July, by Lieutenant General Pavel Rotmistrov's Fifth Guards Tank Army. His T-34s may not have been as power-

Above: A confident German machine-gun team, belonging to Fourth Panzer Army, marches past an abandoned T-34/76 Model 43, its turret reversed. This photograph was taken during the early days of the Kursk offensive, before German troops had met the defences in depth.

Right: A Soviet tank lies abandoned at the roadside. The driver appears to have escaped through the hatch on the glacis plate, but his body, covered by a tarpaulin, bears mute testimony to his fate. Crews faced many dangers, ranging from being burnt alive to being shot.

Right: German soldiers inspect a Soviet Mikoyan-Gurevich MiG-3 fighter, brought down over their lines in central Russia, 1943. The photograph implies that the 'kill' should be credited to the Waffen-SS anti-aircraft machine gun – an MG 34 on a Dreifuss mounting – although there is no guarantee that this was actually the case.

fully armed as the SS Tigers, but there were many more of them and their crews, having waited for just this moment, were willing to move at speed into battle. The result was the biggest tank engagement in history, involving an estimated 1000 armoured fighting vehicles, meeting in an area little more than two miles (3.2km) across.

T-34 crews, aware that they were outgunned by the 88mm main armament of their opponents, drove their tanks forward to close the range, even going so far as to collide with the Tigers to prevent the Germans from manoeuvring into better positions. The sound of armour on armour could be heard for miles around, punctuated by the bark of 76mm or 88mm guns and the explosions that followed.

The battle of attrition

By the end of the day, Fourth Panzer Army's losses since 5 July had reached 350 tanks and around 10,000 men; further north, Ninth Army had lost about 200 tanks and as many as 25,000 casualties. The Soviets had also suffered, but they could afford the losses and could replace them easily from the vast reserves held back to the east of Kursk (it is estimated that the Red Army losses in men and equipment at Kursk were quadruple those suffered by the Germans). Indeed, some of these reserves were committed later on 12 July to mount an attack on Orel, close to the northern shoulder of the salient. This, combined with the news of an Anglo-American assault on Sicily (see Chapter 9), led Hitler to call a halt to the Zitadelle offensive.

Prokhorovka has been described as the 'death ride of the panzers', but this was an epithet that could be applied just as truthfully to the battle as a whole. Zitadelle was virtually the last major tank offensive executed by the Germans during the Second World War – the closest they came thereafter was in the Ardennes in

December 1944, with similar results (see Chapter 10) – and it marked the end of the blitzkrieg era.

As Army Groups Centre and South pulled back from the Kursk area, abandoning both Orel and Belgorod on 5 August, they assumed a defensive posture that soon became the norm as the Soviets mounted a series of relentless attacks all along the Eastern Front. More significantly, these attacks were coordinated and carried out with a new professionalism that was soon to make the Red Army the leading exponent of manoeuvre warfare. Stalin, ably supported by Zhukov, ensured that overwhelming forces were available and were fully capable of defeating the Germans at their own game. The weaknesses of blitzkrieg had been carefully noted – the problems caused by Hitler's constant interference, the yawning gaps between the mechanized spearheads and the foot-slogging infantry, the appalling breakdown of logistic support – and measures taken to make sure that the Red Army did not suffer the same.

By the autumn of 1943, as Kiev and Smolensk were liberated and the last Germans forced back across the River Dniepr, mechanization in the Red Army had been extended to all units involved in the attack and its support, Stalin had delegated operational command to his generals at the front, and supplies had been guaranteed, at least for advances of up to 250 miles (400km). In addition, maskirovka (deception) was being employed to ensure that the enemy was caught by surprise, allowing artillery, armour and motorized infantry to be concentrated in selected 'breakthrough sectors', where advantages of up to 40-to-1 could be attained. Against such sophistication, the Germans could do little, particularly as they were facing simultaneous Allied assaults in the Mediterranean. Hitler's dream was falling apart, leaving the Wehrmacht to face the consequences. On the Eastern Front, the floodgates were about to break.

ITALIAN DEFENCES

The Wehrmacht fought a tenacious and skilful campaign in Italy against an enemy who was both numerically and materially superior. But it was a grim, defensive campaign, a far cry from the tactics of the blitzkrieg.

Left: A young lieutenant (left) issues orders to his NCO against a backdrop of the Italian mountains.

Above: A column of Sturmgeschutz (StuG) IV assault guns, all armed with 75mm StuK 40 guns, in Naples in September 1943.

Once it was obvious that victory would be achieved in North Africa in the spring of 1943, the leaders of the western Allies, Prime Minister Winston Churchill and President Franklin D. Roosevelt, met to discuss their next move. Although the Americans favoured an immediate cross-Channel assault to liberate Northwest Europe, the British were less enthusiastic, recognizing the potential dangers of committing inexperienced troops against the Wehrmacht in France. Instead, Churchill pressed for a Mediterranean strategy, partly to gain experience of amphibious landings, but also because he realized that Italy was a weak link in the Axis alliance. Describing Italy as the 'soft underbelly' of Europe, he envisaged a campaign in Sicily and then on the Italian mainland that would lead to the collapse of Mussolini's dictatorship and the opening up of a new front that would drain German

Above: Soldiers make themselves comfortable among the rocks of a defended position in Italy, 1944. Their shelter is made from the waterproof cape, or Zeltbahn. Usually worn over the uniform, they could be tied together to create a tent.

Right: German troops, aided by naval personnel, arrive in southern Italy in August 1943, having been evacuated from Sicily. The photograph is unusual in showing a German landing craft, which was of little use outside the Mediterranean.

Above: *The crew of a 75mm Panzerabwehrkanone (Pak) 40 anti-tank gun construct a defensive position alongside a village house, Italy, 1944. When they have finished, the position will look like a wooden lean-to to unsuspecting Allied tanks.*

Below: *A tripod-mounted Maschinengewehr (MG) 42 machine gun is prepared for action in southern Italy, 1943. The MG 42, known as the 'Spandau' to Allied troops, had a distinctive 'woodpecker' sound, caused by its rapid rate of fire.*

Above: A 75mm Pak 40 anti-tank gun acquires a target, central Italy, 1944. This particular weapon has not been dug-in or particularly well camouflaged (its position next to a distinctive tree represents a poor choice of ground). It suggests that a hasty defence was required.

Left: A group of German infantrymen, led by their officers and NCOs, marches towards the frontline in Italy, 1944. They seem to be relaxed, implying that Allied forces are not close by; the fact that they are marching in the open by day suggests a lack of Allied air activity.

resources. Hitler's nightmare of a war on two fronts simultaneously in Europe was about to become reality.

The first move was to plan and execute an invasion of Sicily, using the US Seventh and British Eighth Armies from North Africa. Code-named Operation Husky, the invasion began early on 10 July 1943, with landings along a stretch of coast that ran from Syracuse in the east to Licata in the west, supported by airstrikes from Africa and airborne landings to secure key bridges and terrain. Allied intelligence had accurately plotted the main dispositions of the 315,000 Italian and 50,000 German troops on the island, the latter including men who had been withdrawn from North Africa prior to the Allied seizure of Tunis. One of the more powerful formations was the Hermann Göring Division, a Luftwaffe ground unit equipped with Tiger tanks. Some planners predicted a tough campaign.

In the event, the Allied victory was relatively straightforward, despite some hard fighting. The Wehrmacht was stretched to satisfy all the commitments ordered by Hitler in mid-1943 – the build-up for Kursk had taken precedence since March – and no-one was very clear about Italian intentions. These became more apparent on the day of the Allied landings, when Italian units at Licata fled, and by moves in Rome to oust Mussolini two weeks later. By then, however, the Allied armies had established themselves ashore in Sicily and were moving towards their ultimate objective of Messina, close to the southern tip of Italy itself. Recognizing the danger of being trapped, German commanders sought and gained permission to withdraw as many of their men as possible onto the mainland, where more crucial battles were likely to be fought. By 17 August 1943, Sicily was in Allied hands after a campaign lasting 38 days, though 40,000 Germans, 60,000 Italians and much equipment had been successfully evacuated. When this is considered together with concurrent events on the Eastern Front (see Chapter 8), it is apparent that the Wehrmacht was becoming seriously over-stretched.

Below: American prisoners, captured at Anzio in early 1944, are brought to the outskirts of Rome before being paraded through the city in an attempt to intimidate the population with a show of German strength. The tank on the right, which seems to be attracting widespread attention, is a Panther.

Left: A Pz Kpfw VI Ausf H Tiger I of the 508th Heavy Tank Battalion is photographed en route to Aprilia, Italy, 1944. The Tiger I was a very formidable fighting vehicle: with an 88mm KwK 36 gun in the turret and protected by up to 4.3in (110mm) of plate, it was superior to Allied tanks in both armament and armour.

Right: A German gunner carefully sights his 210mm Morser 18 before firing towards Allied lines in central Italy, 1944. Although production shifted to the 170mm Kanone 18 in 1942, the Morser 18 continued to be used throughout the war. Its rate of fire was one round a minute and it had a maximum range of 11.5 miles (18,700m).

Below: A 170mm Kanone 18 heavy artillery piece is about to be fired towards Allied positions at Anzio, early 1944. The K18 first entered service with the German Army in 1941; with a maximum range of 17 miles (28,000m), and a rate of fire of at least 1-2 rounds a minute, it could lay down a devastating bombardment, as the troops at Anzio discovered.

Political events in Italy forced Hitler to turn his attention more firmly to the Mediterranean. Mussolini's overthrow on 25 July brought Marshal Pietro Badoglio to power, and he approached the Allies seeking terms for Italy's surrender. Secret negotiations led to an agreement that the surrender would take effect in early September, coinciding with Allied landings at Reggio, Taranto, Brindisi and Salerno. Italian forces would do nothing to oppose these assaults, opening the way north to Rome and, ultimately, Austria. If this had happened as planned, it would have been disastrous for Germany, leaving its southern flank exposed and compromising all efforts to stall the Soviet advance from the east.

The Wehrmacht takes control

However, Hitler was aware, through his intelligence services, that a surrender was possible and, as soon as it was confirmed, he acted quickly (the Italians were to sign a secret capitulation to the Allies in Sicily on 3 September). Field Marshal Rommel, commander of German troops in northern Italy, disarmed Italian divisions in his sector, while Field Marshal Albrecht Kesselring did the same in the Naples area, close to the projected landing site at Salerno.

Above: Two of the defenders of Anzio, early 1944. Both have adapted their uniforms for comfort and camouflage, implying that they are veterans. The soldier on the left has been issued with an Italian 9mm Beretta M38A submachine gun, known in the Wehrmacht as the Maschinenpistole (Beretta) 38(I).

Thus, when the first Allied units landed at Salerno early on 9 September in Operation Avalanche, they found their passage blocked by elements of General Heinrich von Vietinghoff's Tenth Army, hastily moved south into Italy. Allied divisions belonging to Lieutenant General Mark Clark's US Fifth Army (comprising the US VI Corps and the British X Corps), had to fight hard to establish a beachhead, only to come under pressure from von Vietinghoff's panzers. Between 10 and 18 September, the Salerno landing was in danger of being defeated; it was only after reinforcements had been poured ashore and General Montgomery's Eighth Army had advanced to link up from their landing beaches in the south that the crisis passed. Naples fell to the Allies on 5 October 1943.

Von Vietinghoff's hasty defence of the hills overlooking Salerno was indicative of the problems facing the Allies in Italy. As they

broke out of the beachhead, the Germans pulled back carefully, making use of every obstacle, both natural and man-made, to impede enemy progress. As early as 13 October, Fifth Army had to struggle to cross the River Volturno, only to find another river, the Garigliano, in their way. Further east, Eighth Army were experiencing similar problems on the Rivers Trigno and Sangro. In both sectors, the situation was made worse by the onset of the autumn rains and the fact that the Allies were now approaching the mountainous spine of Italy. The Germans were no more trained or equipped for mountain warfare than their enemies, but they were past masters at spotting the key features from which to mount a defence. By the end of December 1943, the Allied advance had stalled, giving Kesselring, as overall commander-in-chief, time in which to finalize the first of his purpose-built defensive positions – the so-called Gustav Line, stretching from coast to coast through seemingly impassable mountains. A campaign which had begun for the Allies in high hopes of a quick victory was rapidly becoming a grim war of attrition.

The Gustav Line was strongest in the west, covering the approaches to Rome through the Liri Valley. Its central feature was Monte Cassino, towering 1700ft (520m) above the small town of Cassino and topped by a Benedictine monastery, but this was only one aspect of the defences. Dotted around the surrounding mountains, occupying natural strongholds that were sure to be tough to

Right: German infantry pause for a brief rest on their march towards the frontline in Italy, 1944. The motorcyclist and pedal-cyclist are probably messengers, acting as links between this formation and others of its parent unit. All seem to be well equipped and ready to go into battle.

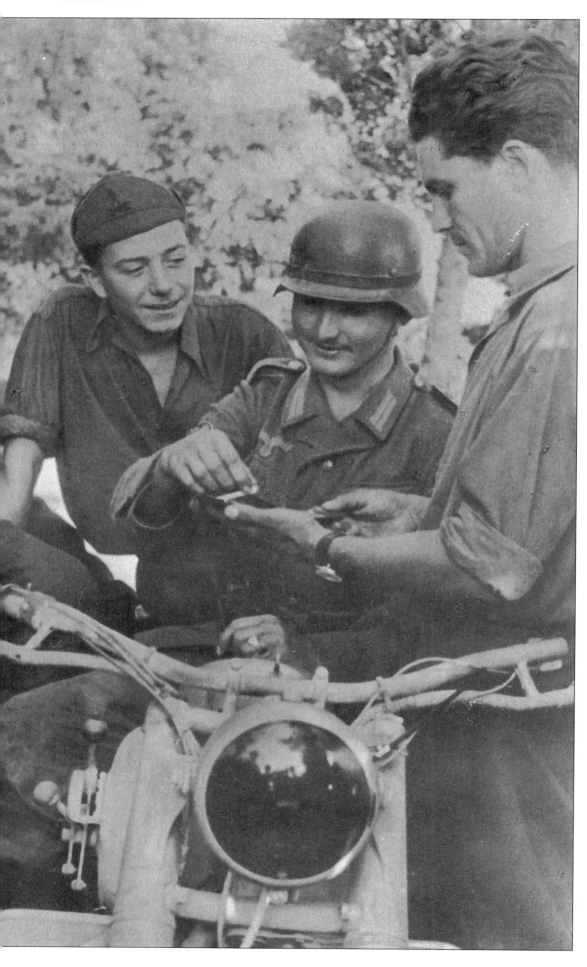

Left: *A German motorcyclist pauses to share a cigarette with Italian soldiers loyal to Benito Mussolini, 1944. After the surrender of Italy in September 1943, some Italian units continued to fight on the Axis side, while others joined the Allies as Co-Belligerent Formations. It was a confusing time.*

Right: *As soon as Hitler was told of the Italian surrender in September 1943, he ordered Italian units to be rounded up and disarmed. A few months later, a column of Italian prisoners of war watches as German troops unpack equipment. The item in the centre on a tripod is an artillery rangefinder.*

Bottom right: *Mines were vital weapons of war in all theatres, but especially in the close fighting in Italy. Here, a German engineer prepares a Schrapnellmine (SMi) 35 anti-personnel mine for use by screwing the igniter to the explosive canister. The SMi 35 could be operated by pressure on the igniter or by tripwire.*

crack, were the troops of Lieutenant General Fridolin von Senger und Etterlin's XIV Panzer Corps. Their title belied their purpose, for they were desperately short of tanks and mobile forces; rather, they depended on infantry, including fully trained paratroops of the Luftwaffe, to block every Allied move and inflict casualties. They proved to be adept at their job.

The Battle of Cassino

The First Battle of Cassino was fought between 17 January and 11 February 1944. Clark, timing his frontal assault to divert German attention away from projected amphibious landings behind the Gustav Line at Anzio, scheduled for 22 January, ordered the British X Corps to seize bridgeheads across the River Garigliano, while the US 34th and 36th Divisions did the same on the River Rapido. Both rivers were wide and difficult to approach, and both were well defended by Wehrmacht units dug in on the northern bank. Von Senger was intent on imposing delays while his main forces finalized their positions closer to Cassino itself, and in this he achieved a measure of success. Although both Allied assaults succeeded in making crossings in the face of appalling weather, they did so at considerable cost, forcing Clark to suspend operations in order to bring up reinforcements.

Meanwhile, the landings at Anzio, code-named Operation Shingle, had taken place as planned. The idea behind them was a

Above: German soldiers fire an MG 42 from a rocky defensive position towards enemy lines, Italy, summer 1944. The machine gunner is using 50-round drum magazines rather than belts of ammunition. The terrain is typical of coastal areas; the mountains of the central spine were far more rugged.

Below: Italian fascist troops, loyal to Mussolini, remove rocks from a mountain road so that the Pz Kpfw III in the background can pass, autumn 1944. The rocks were probably laid by Italian partisans, whose actions often diverted badly-needed Axis troops from the front-line.

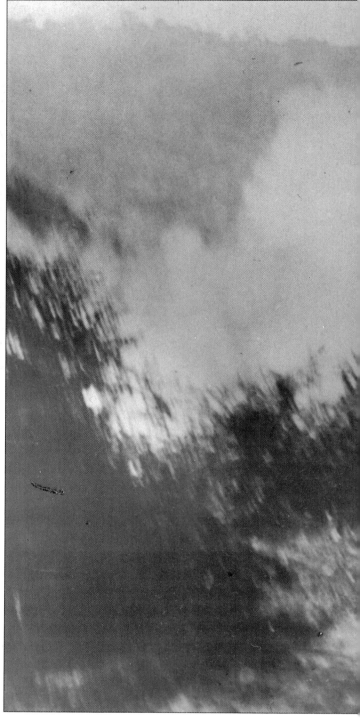

simple one: if Allied units could be projected ashore behind the Gustav Line, German positions would be threatened with encirclement. Faced with simultaneous attacks from the south, von Senger would be forced to pull back, opening the way to Rome. But the practice left much to be desired.

On 22 January 1944, men of the British 1st and US 3rd Divisions, constituting the spearhead of Major General John P. Lucas's US VI Corps, landed without encountering opposition, only to remain static while the build-up took place. For a time, Rome lay exposed, but the opportunity was missed. Elements of General Eberhard von Mackensen's Fourteenth Army were rushed

to the Anzio sector, showing that the Wehrmacht had lost none of its flexibility and mobility, and defensive positions were quickly established to contain the Allied beachhead. What had begun as a militarily logical outflanking operation soon degenerated into bitter head-on fighting.

Lucas finally decided to move forward on 30 January, ordering a two-pronged advance through Cisterna and Campoleone. His troops faced solid opposition. Nor was this purely defensive in nature; on 16 February von Mackensen organized a counter-attack, spearheaded by panzers, that drove a wedge between the British and American sectors, penetrating almost to the coast.

Above: A Sturmgeschutz (StuG) III assault gun opens fire on approaching Allied tanks, central Italy, 1944. Because of their low silhouettes, the StuGs were useful ambush vehicles, although in this case the assault gun appears to have been caught in the open. The dust should allow it to escape.

Allied air and naval strikes saved the day, but it was obvious that the Anzio forces were going nowhere. Lucas was relieved of command and replaced by Major General Lucien K. Truscott, although any chance that this might reverse the situation looked slim. The Wehrmacht was proving adept at defensive warfare.

Above: German mountain troops in a picturesque setting, northern Italy, 1945. They are seated on an Italian L6/40 self-propelled gun - an obsolete weapon but one that is providing mobile firepower to a unit which would otherwise receive none. It was probably confiscated from an Italian unit.

This was reinforced around Cassino, where the mountains had been transformed into a formidable fortress. Although von Senger had deliberately avoided placing units in the historic Benedictine monastery, his paratroops occupied strong positions in Cassino town and among the surrounding hills. On 15 February 1944, as a preliminary to the Second Battle of Cassino, Clark agreed to the bombing of the monastery, believing that it was defended, after which the New Zealand Corps made a direct attack, with French units moving round to the north to assault Monte Belvedere. Relieved of responsibility for preserving the monastery now that the Allies had reduced it to rubble, von Senger extended his line to include that location and committed his few panzers to oppose the New Zealanders. On 20 February, the Allied attack was called off, having achieved little of military value.

The same happened a month later, in the Third Battle of Cassino. Allied aircraft destroyed Cassino town on 15 March, reducing it to ruins, before Clark sent the New Zealanders in again, with predictable results. The only gains were in the surrounding hills, where Allied troops fought desperate hand-to-hand engagements to gain tenuous footholds against German sol-

diers and paratroops who were determined to impose maximum cost. By 25 March, the battle had been closed down.

The Allies break through

Such a costly stalemate could only be broken by Allied firepower and superior numbers, indicating just how far warfare had changed since the flowing blitzkrieg advances by the Wehrmacht in 1940. On 11 May 1944, in the Fourth Battle of Cassino, Clark used all available air and artillery assets to blast German positions, before sending in the maximum number of ground troops. It was effective, for although von Senger's men fought with the tenacity that had come to be expected, they were exhausted and under relentless pressure. French units penetrated the Aurunci Mountains, to the southwest of Cassino, threatening to turn the

Gustav Line, and the Germans began to pull back. On 18 May, Polish troops finally secured the monastery ruins, after which the enemy positions crumbled. This, in turn, allowed the forces at Anzio to secure a breakout, linking up with other elements of the Fifth Army on 26 May. Rome fell on 4 June.

But the German retreat was both orderly and impressive. As von Mackensen's Fourteenth Army, with von Vietinghoff's Tenth on their left, fell back, bridges were destroyed, roads were mined and ambushes laid. The plan, as before in Italy, was to impose delays on the Allies while defensive positions were established further north, this time along the Gothic Line, stretching some 200 miles (320km) from just south of La Spezia on the west coast, running through the Apennines, to Pesaro on the east. Construction had begun in 1943, just before the Germans had pulled out of Sicily, but Kesselring was aware that the longer he could delay his enemy the stronger the fortifications would be. They would also be bolstered by reinforcements from the Eastern Front, promised by Hitler now that his southern flank looked exposed. The fact that the Allies opened a new, even more dangerous front in Normandy on 6 June 1944, made the situation worse. The Wehrmacht was entering the final phase of its existence, squeezed in from every angle.

Kesselring did gain time, however, to finalize the Gothic Line, chiefly because Allied units advancing to the north of Rome and along the east coast of Italy found the going hard. Despite an initial thrust in June of some 90 miles (140km), US and British forces soon encountered stiffening resistance and failed to build up the momentum that might have 'bounced' the German positions.

In August and September 1944, the Allies' Fifth and Eighth Armies mounted a series of limited offensives which began to eat away at the Gothic Line, but in October the autumn rains once more turned the ground to mud and effectively halted all major operations, although the Eighth Army reached Ravenna in a drier spell in December. It would be spring 1945 before they could be resumed. The Wehrmacht, thrust into Italy without a great deal of preparation, had managed to bog the Allies down and stabilize a potentially dangerous situation. It was something they were getting used to having to do.

Below: A German artillery unit in the mountains of central Italy, late 1944. The terrain is well suited to defensive warfare. Note the Italian 6.5mm Mannlicher-Carcano carbine with folding bayonet – known to the Germans as the Karabiner 409(i) – carried by the soldier in the foreground.

DEFEAT IN THE WEST

On 6 June 1944 the Allies landed in Normandy. Under a massive onslaught of men, tanks and aircraft, the Wehrmacht buckled, its understrength divisions conducting a fighting withdrawal to the frontier of Germany itself.

Left: Lieutenant General Karl von Schlieben surrenders to the US 9th Infantry Division, Cherbourg, 26 June 1944.

Above: Field Marshal Erwin Rommel (left), commander of Army Group B in France, inspects the 'Atlantic Wall', 1944.

While Wehrmacht units were fighting desperate battles in Italy and on the Eastern Front in the summer of 1944, a new danger to Germany emerged. On 6 June Allied forces under the overall command of General Dwight D. Eisenhower mounted an amphibious and airborne attack on the coast of Normandy, aiming to destroy the German Army in the west before thrusting through to Berlin. If the situation facing Hitler's troops

had been bad before, it was now approaching catastrophe. A third front in Europe not only increased the pressure but also meant that the Wehrmacht was spread even more thinly. Germany was rapidly approaching the point at which it would simply run out of manpower. By the end of 1944 over 10 million men would be fighting in German uniform, many having been recruited from occupied countries, but there was little left by way of reserves,

Above: Rommel (right), with Field Marshal's baton in his right hand and both the Pour le Mérite and Knight's Cross with Oakleaves and Swords round his neck, inspects a German unit in France, spring 1944. The Allied invasion of Normandy is only weeks away; these soldiers seem to be fit for action.

Right: Field Marshal Gerd von Rundstedt (1875-1953), Commander-in-Chief West, with German officers inspecting defences along the coast of France, 1944. Von Rundstedt was convinced that the Allies would land on the Pas de Calais.

while war-industries were reaching the end of their capability to expand. The Wehrmacht would soon be fighting for the protection of Germany and, ultimately, for its own survival.

German mistakes prior to D-Day

The Normandy landings succeeded for the Allies partly because Hitler was convinced that they were a feint, with the main assault still to come further north along the French coast in the Pas de Calais. As a result, the forces defending Normandy were by no means the best available. With the exception of the 352nd Division, fresh from the Eastern Front, many were second-rate formations manned by non-Germans, while the panzer reserve, which might have had a crucial impact, was held back until it was too late. Even so, the Allies were prevented from seizing all their

Above: *All available weapons were sent to bolster the defences of the Atlantic Wall but, with heavy fighting in the East, only second-rate kit could be spared. An example is this 100mm leichte Feldhaubitze 30(t) – a Czech design.*

Below: *Canadian troops are rounded up on the beach at Dieppe, after the disastrous landing on 19 August 1942. Dieppe cost the Allies over 1000 dead, but the lessons learnt were invaluable when it came to the planning for D-Day.*

objectives on D-Day, enabling Hitler to order some reserve formations forward and allowing those forces in place to mount an effective defence. In this, they were helped by the terrain, something the Wehrmacht was proving adept at exploiting, for in the hinterland of the beachheads, close country known as bocage, together with flooded river estuaries and a network of stone-built villages, offered unique opportunities to delay the Allied advance. The process was by no means easy. The Allies had total air superiority, meaning that virtually every German attempt to move during daylight was costly, but experiences on the Eastern and Italian Fronts, where delaying actions had become the norm, redressed the balance to a significant extent. The fighting in Normandy was guaranteed to be hard.

Left: German gunners manhandle their 105mm leichte Feldhaubitze 18 (Mundungbremse) artillery piece into position on the streets of Cherbourg, June 1944. The gun is a refinement of the normal 105mm leFH 18, with a modified recoil system and muzzle brake to take a stronger charge in the shell.

Below: German soldiers set up a defensive position in Normandy, 1944. The 75mm Panzerabwehrkanone (Pak) 40 is camouflaged, but the choice of a road for the position is odd, suggesting that this may be an exercise, conducted before the Allied invasion. Even so, the men are exposed to air attack.

To begin with, the Allies concentrated on consolidating their beachhead, something the Germans could do little to prevent or disrupt. By 12 June the five original landing beaches – Utah and Omaha in the west, Gold, Juno and Sword in the east – had been linked up. The sole German counter-attack had occurred on 6 June, when 21st Panzer Division advanced out of Caen, only to be halted by naval gunfire. Presented with such a *fait accompli*, Field Marshal von Rundstedt, Commander-in-Chief West, tried to ensure that reserve formations were moved in to contain the bridgehead. Despite disruption to the French rail and road network caused by a combination of Resistance attacks and Allied air interdiction, he enjoyed some success. A British attempt to exploit a perceived gap in the defences at Villers-Bocage was stopped by elements of the 1st SS Panzer Division on 13 June, when Obersturmführer (Lieutenant) Michael Wittmann blunted the spearhead of the British 7th Armoured Division virtually single-handed.

Above: German soldiers carry a wounded comrade past a stone wall towards a field dressing station, Normandy, July 1944. The closeness of the countryside may be appreciated from this photograph. Sunken lanes were a feature of the bocage in Normandy; they helped to stall the Allied breakout.

But there were limits to Wehrmacht capability. While reserve formations concentrated against the British around Caen, seen as the centre of a vital communications network, there was little available to send further west against the Americans. They were able to cut across the Cotentin peninsula by 18 June, taking Cherbourg 11 days later.

Despite this success, however, the Allies were contained. Small German units, often no more than a single tank or anti-tank gun with infantry support, made the most of the bocage, defending a seemingly endless series of small, high-hedged fields which

Above: A Pz Kpfw IV Ausf G occupies a defensive position in a small town in Normandy, July 1944. The tree provides some cover from Allied air observation, although the hastily gathered branches and house-shutters do little to disguise the presence of the tank to ground troops. Perhaps the gun will deter them.

stalled any Allied attempt at breakout. General Montgomery, commanding Allied land forces until Eisenhower's arrival in France in early September, mounted a number of set-piece attacks around Caen, ostensibly to keep the pressure off the Americans so that they could prepare a breakout in their sector, but also in an effort to engage and destroy German formations in a campaign of deliberate attrition. In late June, the British VIII Corps thrust down the Odon Valley in Operation Epsom; in mid-July, Montgomery concentrated his armoured divisions for an advance known as Operation Goodwood, designed to outflank Caen to the east. In both cases, the British enjoyed overwhelming firepower support from artillery, aircraft and even warships; in both cases, they suffered considerable casualties for little territorial gain.

Wehrmacht units, dug in and making the most of the natural defences of the region, not only survived the worst of the gunfire but also showed a remarkable ability to retain their fighting power. In this, they were aided by their weapons, many of which had been developed or refined for just such defensive battles on the Eastern Front. The Panther and Tiger tanks proved superior in both armour and armament to their Allied counterparts; the 88mm anti-aircraft gun, used in the anti-tank role, retained its impact; the

MG42 machine gun and Nebelwerfer multi-barrelled mortar gave the infantry access to sustained fire that could easily disrupt enemy attacks. In the two days of Operation Goodwood, for example, the British lost over 400 tanks in a desperate battle that was characterized by poor inter-arm cooperation and confused command within Montgomery's armoured divisions, characteristics of mobile warfare that the Germans had practised as early as 1940 and were still utilizing four years later, even in defence.

Montgomery was successful in one respect, however. As the battles raged around Caen, German reserves were sucked in, leaving the Americans relatively free to complete their preparations for a breakout in the west. Lieutenant General Omar Bradley, commanding the American sector, planned a general advance towards a line running from Coutances to St Lô and Caumont, after which a concerted drive for Avranches would begin. His troops may

Right: By the summer of 1944, the Allies have complete air superiority over Normandy, forcing German troops to exercise great care during the hours of daylight. One answer is to dig in, building foxholes that are hard to see from the air. This young soldier seems to have the right idea.

Below: A Pz Kpfw II, followed by supply trucks, edges past a traffic problem on a narrow road in Normandy, 1944. A Pz Kpfw VI Tiger I has gone into a ditch; it is taking three schwere Zugkraftwagen 18 heavy artillery tractors (one of which is shown) to tow it out. The group is vulnerable to air attack.

have faced less opposition than the Anglo-Canadians in the east, but the terrain (and weather) was appalling and the Germans were well established in defensive positions. Attempts to drive them out using massive air assaults had some effect, enabling Operation Cobra to begin on 25 July, but the fighting to build up momentum was bitter. Coutances could not be taken until 28 July, followed by Avranches two days later. In these battles the Germans lost 100 precious tanks.

By then, the Wehrmacht in Normandy was beginning to crack, partly under relentless Allied pressure on both flanks but also because of a series of command changes. Hitler sacked von Rundstedt on 1 July, replacing him with Field Marshal von Kluge; on the 17th Field Marshal Rommel, commanding Army Group B in Normandy, was badly injured in an air attack and had to be invalided home. Three days later, on 20 July, Hitler was lucky to survive a bomb explosion in his headquarters at Rastenburg;

was in American hands, the newly arrived US Third Army, commanded by Lieutenant General George S. Patton, was able to advance inland at speed before looping northeast towards the River Seine, threatening German units around Caen with encirclement. Fixed in place by Anglo-Canadian attacks from Caen and Falaise, the bulk of the German Seventh Army, with Fifth Panzer Army in attendance, soon found themselves under attack from all sides in what became known as the Falaise Pocket, Although the neck of the pocket was not closed until 20 August 1944, about 60,000 bedraggled Wehrmacht troops were trapped inside, along with thousands of trucks and 500 armoured vehicles; under heavy air and artillery fire, more than 10,000 were killed before the remainder surrendered.

France is liberated

By then, the Allies had opened up yet another front in Operation Dragoon, an amphibious and airborne assault on the coast of southern France which quickly led to an advance up the Rhône Valley against weak German resistance. In the north, Paris was liberated on 25 August and, as Allied formations advanced into Belgium and towards the German frontier, linking up with the Dragoon invaders, most of France was cleared.

Left: German gunners earn their pay, holding down the trails of 100mm leichte Feldhaubitze 18 (Mundungbremse) artillery pieces as they are fired from a concrete pier during the Allied invasion of southern France in August 1944. The recoil must be vicious.

Below: Soldiers load 88mm Raketenpanzerbuchse 54 anti-tank rocket launchers into a camouflaged staff car, Normandy, July 1944. The RPzB 54, known as the Panzerschreck, was a copy of the American 'Bazooka', but more devastating in its impact. In the terrain of Normandy it was an ideal ambush weapon.

when he discovered that this was the result of a plot among disaffected army officers, he instigated a purge which removed key commanders throughout the Wehrmacht. Command cohesion, already weakened by enormous officer casualties on all fronts, was significantly undermined.

These problems, coupled with the Allied ability to out-produce the Germans in terms of numbers of weapons, meant that the Normandy battle could have only one outcome. Once Avranches

Above: An American soldier (left) views the devastated remains of a German column, caught in the open by Allied aircraft, Falaise Pocket, August 1944. The wrecks have been pushed aside to clear the road, implying that the battle has moved on, but the bodies have yet to be buried.

The Wehrmacht faced disaster but, as so often before, recovered with remarkable speed. As the Allies advanced, they stretched their supply lines to breaking point and came across hardening enemy resistance the closer they came to Germany itself. In addition, the weather was beginning to change, promising rain and mud that would prevent momentum. Montgomery, now commanding 21st Army Group, persuaded Eisenhower to allow an airborne assault in his sector, designed to seize key bridges in southern Holland that would then be linked together by ground forces, but the operation, code-named Market Garden, failed to achieve all its objectives. Although US airborne divisions secured bridges across the Wilhelmina Canal north of Eindhoven

Left: An image of the stress of battle: a German soldier, still clutching his rifle, takes the opportunity to eat an apple taken from an orchard in Normandy, August 1944. His vacant eyes have what the Americans would call 'the 1000-yard stare'.

Right: Once the Allies had broken out from the Normandy beachhead in August 1944, the Germans were forced to retreat. A combination of weather and Allied logistic problems allowed them to recover.

Above: 75mm shells are loaded aboard a Sturmgeschutz (StuG) III Ausf G from a truck near Mortain, Normandy, August 1944. Hitler ordered his panzer forces to mount a counter-attack against the US breakout in August, aiming to sever their line at Mortain. It failed, wasting German resources at a key moment.

Left: German infantry set up their 80mm Granatwerfer 34 mortar in the close country of the Normandy bocage, July 1944. The 80mm GrW 34 was a sturdy and accurate weapon, capable of firing up to 25 rounds a minute in the hands of an experienced crew. It proved deadly in the bocage fighting.

Right: British prisoners of war, captured on Hill 112 during Operation Epsom in late June 1944, are marched away under escort. They have just been involved in a bitter battle, called off when British commanders in Normandy were informed via Enigma decrypts that substantial German reinforcements were on their way.

Above: Three German soldiers, survivors of the Falaise Pocket, contemplate their fortunes, August 1944. Their eyes say it all – they have seen death and destruction on an awesome scale, as Allied fighter-bombers and artillery bombarded formations of the German Seventh Army encircled in Normandy. Over 10,000 of their comrades are dead.

and the Rivers Maas and Waal at Grave and Nijmegen, the British 1st Airborne Division was pushed too far forward, to seize bridges across the Lower Rhine at Arnhem, and had to be withdrawn. In addition, two SS panzer divisions, recuperating in the Arnhem sector from the Normandy battles, mounted an effective defence, preventing the link-up by elements of the British XXX Corps.

Eisenhower's broad front

Once this battle was over towards the end of September, Eisenhower insisted on conducting a more measured advance towards the German frontier and, eventually, the barrier of the River Rhine. German recovery enabled the Wehrmacht to take advantage of the autumn rains to stall Allied progress. By November 1944, the war in the west appeared to have reached a temporary stalemate. Most Allied commanders resigned themselves to a renewed campaign in the spring. The Wehrmacht, meanwhile, was desperately trying to scrape together replacements for the units that had been lost up to that point.

The Allies underestimated their enemy. As early as September, Hitler had noted that the two US armies that made up General Bradley's 12th Army Group were advancing on divergent axes, split by the thinly held Ardennes. In desperate need to blunt the Allied advance in the west in order to concentrate reserves in the east, where Soviet attacks were apparently limitless (see Chapter 11), the Führer planned to use massed panzer formations to strike through the Ardennes, cross the Meuse as they had done in 1940, and recapture Brussels and Antwerp. This would split Allied armies in two and force Eisenhower onto the defensive, delaying the assault on Germany from the west. Code-named Wacht am Rhein (Watch on the Rhine), the operation was prepared in great secrecy, partly to gain surprise and partly because Hitler no longer trusted many of his army commanders. It was also planned for mid-December 1944, when winter weather would ground Allied aircraft and give the panzers at least a chance of success. By 15

December a total of 25 divisions, 10 of them armoured, had been concentrated into an area between Monschau in the north and Echternach in the south; 275,000 German troops and nearly 1000 armoured vehicles were facing less than 83,000 Americans and about 420 tanks.

The Ardennes Offensive

The attack began on 16 December and achieved surprise. Denied air cover because of overcast skies, the Americans could do little to prevent a breakthrough, although sufficient numbers held out in small isolated groups to deny an early build-up of German speed. Kampfgruppe Peiper, the unit spearheading the advance in the north, made significant progress along the Amblève Valley, while further south elements of the reconstituted Fifth Panzer Army destroyed American units on the Schnee Eifel, threatening the key road centres at St Vith and Bastogne. However, success was short-lived.

Eisenhower, unlike Allied commanders in 1940, did not panic, preferring to contain the German advance by committing reserve

Bottom left: *German mountain troops rest in a vineyard in southern France before advancing to face Allied forces that have landed in Operation Dragoon, August 1944. The men have only just arrived from Italy and they must know that there is little they can do to stop the Allies. The Wehrmacht is over-stretched.*

Below: *As the weather begins to break, German infantry trudge wearily through northern France, away from the advancing Allies. The Pz Kpfw V Panther is covering their retreat, making the most of overcast skies to come out into the open, confident that no enemy aircraft will be flying.*

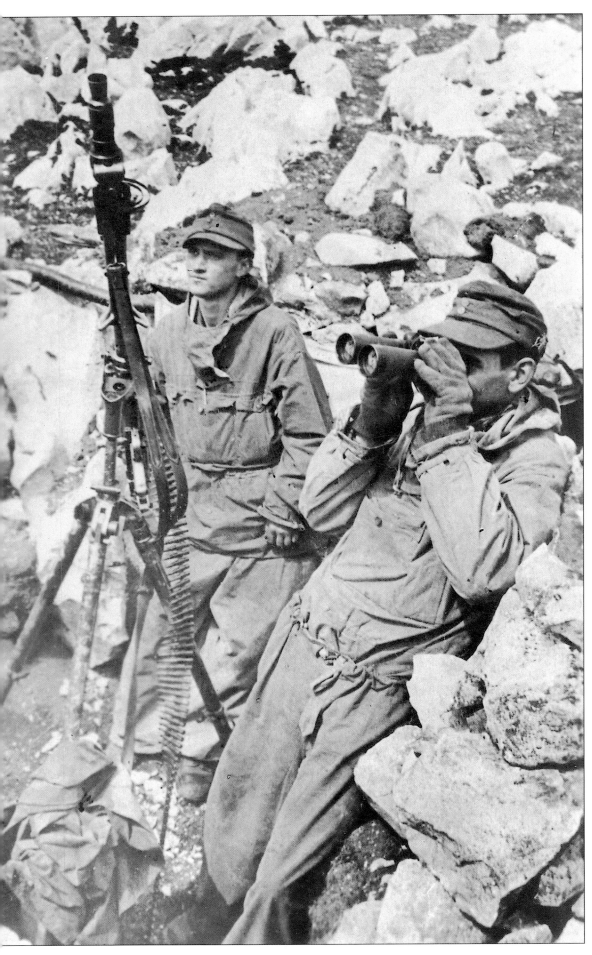

Left: German mountain troops keep a watchful eye out for Allied aircraft while occupying a position in the foothills of the French Alps, August 1944. Their machine gun is on a lightweight Dreifuss AA mounting. Note the distinctive metal Edelweiss badge on the Mountain Hat (Gebirgsmutze) of the soldier on the right.

Top right: A light anti-aircraft gun, carefully camouflaged, provides some protection to these troops, dug-in amid fairly desolate terrain in the Saar region, autumn 1944. The trenches are reminiscent of the Western Front in World War I; all that is missing is mud – and that will soon be added in abundance.

Bottom right: Formidable firepower awaits the Allies in the Saar, autumn 1944. The machine gun is an MG 42 and behind it lurks a Pak 40 anti-tank gun; both are ready for action. The photograph is clearly posed, but it does indicate that the Wehrmacht still had sharp teeth even this late in the war.

Right: The four-man crew of an 80mm Granatwerfer 34 mortar shield themselves from the noise as a round is fired. The loader reaches for another shell, ready to maintain the bombardment of American positions in the Ardennes, December 1944.

Below: German supply vehicles struggle through the snow to support the offensive in the Ardennes (the 'Battle of the Bulge'), December 1944. The scene may be picturesque, but it hides an awful truth about the Wehrmacht by this time – it is just incapable of keeping its front-line forces adequately supplied.

formations to its northern and southern shoulders, helping to create a 'bulge' in the Ardennes which could then be squeezed out. At the same time, he sent forces to protect St Vith and Bastogne, creating rocks in the stream of the enemy assault and so breaking up the panzer momentum. When it is added that the panzers themselves were running out of fuel and ammunition after less than two days, and that Allied airpower reappeared over the battle area once the weather began to clear, the chances of German success can be seen to have been slim.

Watch on the Rhine fails

St Vith held out until 21 December, by which time Eisenhower had packed reserves along the northern shoulder and ordered Patton, in the south, to turn 90 degrees to his left to link up with Bastogne, about to be surrounded and besieged. Patton achieved the link on 26 December. Although some hard fighting was still to come, the Germans had effectively shot their bolt.

As Allied divisions advanced into the bulge from north and south, joining up at Houffalize on 15 January 1945, Hitler had no choice but to withdraw his battered formations. Over 120,000 German troops were lost, together with most of their equipment. Far from delaying the Allied advance towards the Rhine and into Germany, Hitler's offensive had eased the way. The Wehrmacht could not afford to lose many more men, especially as the Soviets were pushing from the east. The war was approaching its end.

Right: As German formations are poised to mount their counter-attack in the poorly defended Ardennes region, a forward observer uses powerful binoculars, camouflaged to blend in with the surrounding rocks of his position, to make a last-minute check. All is quiet – the Americans are about to be caught by surprise.

Left: German motorcyclists find the going difficult along a snow-covered track in the Ardennes, late December 1944. Troops such as these were used by the panzer spearheads as their 'eyes and ears', scouting far ahead and to the flanks in an effort to find a way through the unforgiving terrain.

CHAPTER 11

THE END OF THE GERMAN ARMY

On the Eastern Front, following the failure at Kursk, the Wehrmacht was forced onto the defensive after July 1943, and its armies were thrown back to the gates of Berlin by a series of relentless Soviet hammer blows.

Left: A crude birchwood cross, topped by a battle-damaged helmet, stands as mute testimony to a dead German soldier.

Above: German troops, with their officer (right), seek shelter from the weather in a bunker close to the Rhine, late 1944.

By the beginning of 1944, Soviet troops were firmly on the offensive, gradually overwhelming and out-fighting their enemies in a succession of operations that were relentless in their ferocity and sequence. In January, the siege of Leningrad, conducted for nearly 900 days at an estimated cost of one million Soviet lives, was broken, forcing elements of Army Group North to pull back to the west. Further south, in the Ukraine, Army Group South and Army Group A were shattered by pincer attacks that trapped more than 60,000 German troops in the Korsun 'pocket'; a breakout was attempted in mid-February, but more than half the beleaguered forces were lost. Nor were the survivors allowed any rest. In early March, ignoring the mud of the spring

Above: *German infantry, still reasonably well equipped, pull back towards the Rhine after the abortive Ardennes attack, January 1945. They are passing a ditched Panzerjäger VI Elefant, a powerful tank-hunter created by mounting an 88mm Pak 43 anti-tank gun on a Porsche Tiger chassis.*

Right: *In a desperate attempt to slow Soviet advances in the East, German engineers prepare to destroy a railway bridge over the Niemen River at Grodno in Poland in 1944. They are priming detonator-cord circuits, attached to the captured Soviet explosives packed inside the bridge structure.*

thaw, the Soviets renewed their offensive, pushing the Germans back across the River Bug. The Seventeenth Army, left isolated in the Crimea, was destroyed in April and May, by which time the defences on the Bug had been breached, Odessa had fallen and Soviet forces had entered Rumania, threatening the Balkans.

These Soviet advances left Army Group Centre occupying an enormous salient around four key locations – Vitebsk, Orsha, Mogilev and Bobruysk. Despite its obvious vulnerability, Hitler refused to reinforce the salient, preferring to send troops to pro-

Above: German soldiers, happy to have escaped the Soviet hordes even though they have lost most of their equipment, pause to eat from tins hastily converted into food containers. They will not be able to rest for long; the Soviet advances by early 1945 were relentless, taking vast swathes of territory.

Right: Engineers prepare to demolish the stone towers of a river bridge on the Eastern Front, early 1945. A number of Tellermine 42 anti-tank mines have been strung together, with the intention of undermining the foundations of the structure. They are likely to be effective, although the enemy will not be stopped.

tect the Hungarian and Rumanian oilfields. This left Army Group Centre with less than 500,000 men to hold a front over 650 miles (1000km) long. Against this, the Soviets concentrated four Fronts, totalling about 1.2 million soldiers, 4000 armoured fighting vehicles and 6000 aircraft, planning a massive blow that would eject the Germans from Soviet territory and into eastern Poland. Code-named Operation Bagration, it began on 22 June 1944.

The Wehrmacht could do little to prevent its success. Deceived as to the nature, timing and location of the assault, German units were spread thinly and were quickly overwhelmed, particularly in the specially designated 'breakthrough sectors' into which the Soviets concentrated the bulk of their forces. Vitebsk fell on 27 June, for a loss of about 30,000 German troops; Mogilev and

Right: By 1945, the German Army was desperately short of transport vehicles and, more especially, petrol to fuel them. In such circumstances, any form of motive power was sought, as this photograph suggests. The oxen have been hitched to a 3.7 cm Pak 35/36 anti-tank gun, itself a hopelessly outclassed weapon.

Left: Germany begins to reap the whirlwind: a group of infantrymen trudge through the shattered streets of a town in Saxony, hit by Soviet artillery fire, 1945. After nearly four years of fighting on the Eastern Front, the Germans are now learning the harsh reality of defeat, seeing their own country devastated.

Bobruysk followed within 48 hours, costing Army Group Centre a further 50,000 men. The next Soviet objective was Minsk, liberated on 3 July, after which elements of the 3rd Belorussian Front thrust northwest to take Vilnius and threaten Riga, cutting the communication and supply lines to Army Group North.

The Red Army reaches the Vistula

Further south, Lvov fell on 27 July, enabling the 1st Belorussian Front to advance as far as the River Vistula, less than eight miles from Warsaw. Resistance fighters of the Polish Home Army took the opportunity to rise in revolt against the Germans, only to find that the Soviets had stalled, partly because they had outrun their supply lines but also, it is suspected, because Stalin was quite content to see the Poles crushed before he occupied their country. The Germans obliged in August and September 1944, razing Warsaw to the ground in a bitter act of repression. Soviet troops were to go no further in the central sector until January 1945, although operations did continue to clear Estonia, Latvia and Lithuania, further isolating Army Group North.

Meanwhile, offensives elsewhere had left the Wehrmacht with no chance to recover. On 20 August, the 2nd and 3rd Ukrainian

Right: Soldiers hitch a lift on the Eastern Front. The vehicle is a Sturmgeschutz (StuG) III Ausf G mobile command post, as indicated by the aerial and the stowage bin on the back to house kit displaced by a large radio set inside. Note also the extra wide 'winter' tracks and the armoured skirt.

Left: Infantrymen stare at the devastation around them as they move through a German city hit by a Soviet artillery bombardment, early 1945. The Soviets placed great emphasis on their artillery, massing it in overwhelming numbers to ensure the complete destruction of targets. The effect on German Army morale was severe.

Fronts attacked deep into Rumania, trapping the German Sixth Army (re-raised since Stalingrad) and triggering far-reaching political changes in the Balkans. Later in the same month, King Michael of Rumania switched sides, declaring war on Germany and seeking terms from Stalin. In early September Bulgaria, which had never declared war on the Soviet Union, was given no choice but to accept Soviet occupation. Only in Hungary, where Hitler ensured a degree of loyalty by overthrowing the existing Regent

and replacing him with the fascist leader Ferenc Szalasi, did resistance harden, although by early November, Soviet troops were laying siege to Budapest (it would stubbornly hold out until mid-February 1945). Other Soviet units marched through Bulgaria to link up with Tito's communist Partisans in northern Yugoslavia in October, threatening Axis forces in Greece and Albania with isolation. They withdrew as quickly as they could, leaving most of the Balkans clear.

Below left: *German light tanks, the one nearest the camera having suffered damage to its right-hand track guard, move forward in a last-ditch effort to halt the Soviet advance into the Fatherland, 1945. The tanks appear to be modified versions of the Pz Kpfw 38(t), an obsolete design in 1940, let alone 1945.*

Above: *By 1945, some Wehrmacht units could still pack a powerful punch, as these Pz Kpfw VI Tiger Is, moving through a damaged town in Germany, imply. But there were never enough to go round and those that did survive often lacked fuel and spare parts. The days of fast-moving blitzkrieg were long gone.*

Thus, by January 1945, with the concurrent failure of the counter-attack through the Ardennes (see Chapter 10), the Wehrmacht was being squeezed on two fronts simultaneously. As offensive followed offensive, vast tracts of occupied territory had been lost and each defeat had seen the destruction of enormous quantities of irreplaceable equipment, together with the capture or death of hundreds of thousands of equally irreplaceable men. Those who remained faced enemies with seemingly limitless supplies and growing military skills, particularly on the Eastern Front, where Soviet operational techniques had reached high levels of sophistication and effect.

This was shown on 12 January, when two assaults cracked the Eastern Front apart. In the north, Soviet troops advanced towards Danzig, severing the links between the remains of Army Group Centre and its bases in Germany; about 500,000 men were trapped with their backs to the sea. Some were saved by the German Navy, but they took no further part in the war. At the same time, a major Soviet offensive broke out of bridgeheads on the Vistula to isolate Warsaw and advance at great speed towards the River Oder, less than 50 miles (80km) from Berlin. The only stubborn German resistance occurred in and around Poznan, designated a 'fortress city' by Hitler and defended by a mixture of old men and young boys of the *Volkssturm* (Home Guard), armed with little more than one-shot panzerfaust anti-tank weapons. They did not last long, being overwhelmed by 23 February – the end of the war was fast approaching.

Above: A panzertruppe NCO instructs a member of the Hitlerjugend (Hitler Youth) in the intricacies of the single-shot Panzerfaust 60 anti-tank weapon. As the Allies swept in from east and west in 1945, the use of such youngsters and weapons was an indication of the desperate plight of the Nazi regime.

By then, Anglo-American forces in the west had resumed their offensive towards the Rhine. Eisenhower, as Supreme Commander, was intent on a broad-front advance that would take his armies to the west bank of the river in unison, after which Montgomery's 21st Army Group would mount an assault crossing in the north, with subsidiary crossings further south by the Americans. The aim at this stage was still to take Berlin from the west, although the main task in February and early March 1945 was actually to close to the Rhine. This was done by means of a series of offensives.

In the north, in Operation Veritable, Anglo-Canadian formations attacked on 8 February, making good progress until they encountered the forests of the Reichswald, stoutly defended by hardened veterans of General Alfred Schlemm's First Parachute Army. They made extensive use of the terrain to slow the Allied advance, aided immeasurably by extremely wet weather that

turned the forest and its approaches to mud. Gradually forced back by overwhelming firepower, Schlemm's army retained its cohesion, withdrawing across the Rhine between Emmerich and Xanten in late February, blowing up the bridges behind them.

Operation Grenade, an assault further south by the US Ninth Army which was meant to be concurrent, was delayed by flooding and did not even begin until 23 February. However, German reserves had already been committed to counter Veritable so the Americans experienced less stubborn resistance. They reached the Rhine near Düsseldorf on 1 March.

To their south, Bradley's 12th Army Group advanced on a broad front to take the area from Cologne to Koblenz in Operation Lumberjack, during which, on 7 March, German defenders of the Ludendorff railway bridge across the Rhine at Remagen were surprised by elements of the US 9th Armored Division. As infantry rushed across, capturing the bridge intact,

Below: Members of the Volkssturm ('Home Guard') in a German city designated a Festung (fortress) by Hitler, take instruction in how to operate the Panzerfaust. Theirs is a desperate plight – even if they manage to fire a single projectile and destroy a tank, they will be overwhelmed by other forces.

Germans all along the front were dealt a demoralizing blow: the natural barrier of the Rhine, described by Nazi propaganda as impregnable, had been broken with apparent ease. It was indicative of the over-stretch that the Wehrmacht was subject to – the bridge had been defended by less than 400 men, many of them locally raised Volkssturm – but it also showed how close to collapse the Reich really was. Hitler's predictable response was to order the court-martial and execution of those officers deemed responsible for the loss of the bridge, a policy that was already the norm throughout Wehrmacht rear areas. It was a sure sign that the end for Germany was near.

Target Berlin

By the end of March, the western Allies were on the banks of the Rhine all along its length, the southern sector having been seized by Lieutenant General Jacob Devers's Franco-American 6th Army Group, with Patton's US Third Army in attendance, in Operation Undertone. Eisenhower agreed to Bradley's request for reinforcements at Remagen, and Patton made sure that his army stayed in the headlines by seizing crossings at Oppenheim on 22/23 March, but the emphasis remained with Montgomery in the north. Late on

Above: German plenipotentiaries sign the articles of unconditional surrender at SHAEF headquarters at Reims, 7 May 1945. In the centre, reading the documents, is General Alfred Jodl (1890-1946), chief of operations at OKW; he is flanked by his ADC and Admiral Hans Georg von Friedeburg (1895-1945).

23 March, under an artillery bombardment of more than 2000 guns, British, Canadian and American infantry under Montgomery's command mounted an amphibious assault between Rees and Orsoy. Once established on the east bank, they were joined by airborne troops, the arrival of whom broke the German resistance. By the end of the month, Montgomery had 20 divisions and over 1000 tanks across the river and was itching to advance on Berlin.

He was stopped by Eisenhower, who was aware that political decisions made at Yalta, where the 'Big Three' (Churchill, Roosevelt and Stalin) had met in February, had given the task of taking the German capital to the Soviets. The western and eastern Allies were to meet on the River Elbe, to the west of Berlin, leaving Montgomery to liberate northern Holland and seize the Ruhr industrial region, already effectively isolated by Rhine crossings at

Above: Members of the Wehrmacht march into captivity, in this case American. They were lucky; most of those who surrendered to the Russians would never see Germany again. Despite their efforts, the Third Reich had perished – a just reward for the army's enthusiastic embrace of National Socialism.

Wesel and Remagen. The decision shifted the emphasis of the western advance to Bradley and Devers, who were ordered to thrust deep into central and southern Germany, where it was rumoured that hard-line Nazi units were intent on creating strongholds in the Alps. Patton, under Bradley's command, released his armour in a spectacular burst of speed that took it to the borders of Austria and Czechoslovakia by late April.

The Wehrmacht was collapsing rapidly. On the Eastern Front, Soviet troops took Budapest in mid-February and virtually destroyed the cream of the Waffen-SS panzer divisions around Lake Balaton in early March, opening the way to the Hungarian oilfields. Hitler's anger manifested itself in an order for all SS officers involved to be stripped of their decorations, something that dealt a mortal blow to their morale. As German defences in the Balkan sector fell apart, other Soviet units entered Austria, seizing Vienna on 6 April, and advanced northwest towards Prague. Each offensive destroyed another Wehrmacht army that could have defended Berlin.

Nor were the disasters confined to the Western and Eastern Fronts. On 1 April 1945, Allied troops in northern Italy resumed the offensive that had been stopped by winter weather a few months earlier (see Chapter 9). The initial attack took place on the east coast of Italy, where the British Eighth Army initiated a tough battle to seize the flooded shores of Lake Comacchio before advancing northwest across the Rivers Senio and Santerno. Once

the Germans were engaged in this sector, the US Fifth Army drove north towards Bologna, linking up with the British on the outskirts of that city on 20 April before pursuing von Vietinghoff's broken army across the River Po. On 29 April, representatives of the German forces still intact signed an unconditional surrender, to come into effect on 2 May. It was the first front to collapse, enabling Allied units to move up to the Alps and make contact with American forces from the Rhine.

By then, the ultimate battle – for Berlin – had been fought. Marshal Zhukov, commanding the 1st Belorussian Front, began his attack from the River Oder towards the city on 16 April with 193 divisions against 50 weak German ones, while other Soviet formations to his north and south thrust deep into Germany, making contact with Anglo-American troops along the Elbe and in Czechoslovakia. Berlin was defended by a series of fortified lines, the first of which, on the Seelow Heights, fell on 17 April after exceptionally heavy fighting. What remained of the Wehrmacht was no longer fighting for Hitler or Nazi ideology but for its life. Reports from those areas of Germany already under Soviet occupation spoke of unrestrained looting, murder and rape, while the fate of German soldiers unfortunate enough to fall into Soviet hands was well known. Despite shortages of reserves, petrol, ammunition and even basic weapons, the defenders of Berlin exacted a terrible price on their attackers as they fought for each fortified line and then for every street and building.

The Third Reich collapses

The final Soviet offensive began on 26 April, squeezing the last of the garrison into a corridor less than three miles (five kilometres) across and 10 miles (16km) long. This was then severed and the resultant pockets destroyed. Late on 30 April the German parliament building, the Reichstag, was taken, symbolizing the end of the Nazi state. Hitler was already dead – he committed suicide in the Führerbunker beneath his Chancellory at about 1530 hours on the 30th – and his few remaining soldiers, demoralized, bitter and afraid, could do no more. On 2 May, the remnants of the Berlin garrison surrendered, having inflicted an estimated 100,000 casualties on the Soviets since 16 April. However, that was nothing compared to the total losses suffered by the Wehrmacht on the Eastern Front since June 1941: 1,015,000 dead.

A few isolated pockets of German troops had still to be mopped up, but many were trying desperately to march west, towards Anglo-American lines, before surrendering (during the month of April 1945, the Western Allies took 1,650,000 prisoners, taking the total since the campaign started in June 1944 to almost 3,000,000). The war in Europe officially ended on 8 May. The Wehrmacht ceased to exist, having lost an estimated 3.5 million men since the start of hostilities in 1939. Despite its stunning victories in the early years and its dogged defence of key locations to the end, it had achieved nothing of lasting value, having fought for a discredited and immoral cause. Its enormous skill and bravery had been wasted.

INDEX

PICTURE CREDITS

Christopher Ailsby Historical Archives: 42 (t), 42 (b), 43, 44, 50 (b), 53 (t), 55 (t), 55 (b), 58, 107 (b), 109 (t), 110 (b), 111, 112 (t), 112 (b), 113, 114 (t), 114 (b), 115, 119 (b), 123 (t), 126 (b), 127, 170 (t), 170 (b), 171, 172 (t), 172 (b)

Leszek Erenfeicht via Espadon Books Ltd: 18, 19, 20 (t), 20 (b), 21 (t), 21 (b), 22, 23 (t), 23 (b), 24, 24-25, 25, 26, 27 (t), 28 (t), 28 (b), 28-29, 30 (t), 32, 36, 37 (b), 38, 39, 40 (b), 41 (b), 45 (t), 45 (b), 46, 48, 50 (t), 51 (b), 52, 53 (b), 54-55, 56 (t), 56 (b), 58-59, 60, 61, 62-63, 63 (t), 63 (b), 64, 65, 66 (t), 66 (b), 67 (t), 67 (b), 68 (t), 68 (b), 69 (t), 70, 71 (b), 72, 73 (t), 73 (b), 74 (t), 74 (b), 75, 76 (t), 76 (b), 77, 78-79, 79 (t), 79 (b), 80 (t), 80 (b), 81, 82 (t), 82 (b), 82-83, 84, 85, 87 (b), 88, 89 (t), 89 (b), 90 (t), 90 (b), 91, 92-93, 93 (t), 93 (b), 94 (t), 94 (b), 95, 96, 97 (t), 97 (b), 98-99, 100, 101 (t), 101 (b), 102 (t), 102 (b), 103 (t), 106 (t), 107 (t), 108, 109 (b), 110 (t), 118 (b), 119, 120 (t), 121, 123 (b), 124 (b), 126 (t), 128, 129, 130 (t), 130 (b), 131 (t), 131 (b), 132 (t), 132 (b), 133, 134 (t), 134 (b), 135, 136, 137 (t), 137 (b), 138, 139 (t), 139 (b), 140 (t), 140 (b), 140-141, 142, 143, 146 (t), 146 (b), 147 (t), 147 (b), 148 (t), 148 (b), 149, 150, 151 (t), 151 (b), 152-153, 153, 154, 155, 156, 157 (t), 157 (b), 158 (t), 158 (b), 159, 160, 162 (tl), 162 (tr), 162 (b), 163, 165, 166 (t), 166 (b), 167 (t), 167 (b), 168, 168-169, 169

Private collection: 1, 2, 6, 7, 9 (t), 10 (t), 12, 13 (t), 13 (b), 14 (t), 14 (b), 17 (t), 27 (b), 30 (b), 33 (b), 34-35, 37 (t), 106 (b), 164

TRH Pictures: 8, 9 (b), 10 (b), 11, 15, 16, 17 (b), 31, 33 (t), 35 (t), 35 (b), 40 (t), 41 (t), 47, 49, 51 (t), 57, 69 (b), 71 (t), 86 (t), 86 (b), 87 (t), 103 (b), 104, 105, 116, 117, 118 (t), 120 (b), 122, 124 (t), 125, 144, 145, 154-155, 161 (t), 161 (b), 174